THE BEST **JIGS & FIXTURES FOR YOUR WOODSHOP**

POPULAR WOODWORKING BOOKS

CINCINNATI, OHIO
www.popularwoodworking.com

D1402974

Read This Important Safety Notice

To prevent accidents, keep safety in mind while you work. Use the safety guards installed on power equipment; they are for your protection. When working on power equipment, keep fingers away from saw blades, wear safety goggles to prevent injuries from flying wood chips and sawdust, wear headphones to protect your hearing, and consider installing a dust vacuum to reduce the amount of airborne sawdust in your woodshop. Don't wear loose clothing, such as neckties or shirts with loose sleeves, or jewelry, such as rings, necklaces or bracelets, when working on power equipment. Tie back long hair to prevent it from getting caught in your equipment. People who are sensitive to certain chemicals should check the chemical content of any product before using it. The authors and editors who compiled this book have tried to make the contents as accurate and correct as possible. Plans, illustrations, photographs and text have been carefully checked. All instructions, plans and projects should be carefully read, studied and understood before beginning construction. In some photos, power tool guards have been removed to more clearly show the operation being demonstrated. Always use all safety guards and attachments that come with your power tools. Due to the variability of local conditions, construction materials, skill levels, etc., neither the author nor Popular Woodworking Books assumes any responsibility for any accidents, injuries, damages or other losses incurred resulting from the material presented in this book. Prices listed for supplies and equipment were current at the time of publication and are subject to change. Glass shelving should have all edges polished and must be tempered. Untempered glass shelves may shatter and can cause serious bodily injury. Tempered shelves are very strong and if they break will just crumble, minimizing personal injury.

Metric Conversion Chart

TO CONVERT	TO	MULTIPLY BY
Inches	Centimeters	2.54
Centimeters	Inches	0.4
Feet	Centimeters	30.5
Centimeters	Feet	0.03
Yards	Meters	0.9
Meters	Yards	1.1
Sq. Inches	Sq. Centimeters	6.45
Sq. Centimeters	Sq. Inches	0.16
Sq. Feet	Sq. Meters	0.09
Sq. Meters	Sq. Feet	10.8
Sq. Yards	Sq. Meters	0.8
Sq. Meters	Sq. Yards	1.2
Pounds	Kilograms	0.45
Kilograms	Pounds	2.2
Ounces	Grams	28.4
Grams	Ounces	0.035

Visit our Web site at www.popularwoodworking.com for information on more resources for woodworkers.

Other fine Popular Woodworking Books are available from your local bookstore or direct from the publisher.

08   07   06   05   04   5   4   3   2

Library of Congress Cataloging-in-Publication Data

The best jigs & fixtures for your woodshop / from the editor of Popular woodworking.--1st ed.
    p. cm.
    Includes index.
    ISBN 1-55870-611-9 (alk. paper)
    1. Woodworking tools--Design and construction. 2. Woodwork--Equipment and supplies--Design and construction. 3. Jigs and fixtures--Design and construction. I. Title: Best jigs and fixtures for your woodshop. II. Popular Woodworking Books (Firm). III. Popular woodworking.

TT186.B473 2004
684'.08--dc21

ACQUISITIONS EDITOR: Jim Stack
EDITED BY: Jennifer Ziegler
DESIGNED BY: Brian Roeth
LAYOUT ARTIST: Kathy Gardner
PRODUCTION COORDINATED BY: Mark Griffin

ACKNOWLEDGEMENTS

This book was conceived with the idea of having our readers and fellow woodworkers send us their best and/or favorite woodworking jigs and fixtures. We received several submissions and chose first, second and third place winners.

The first place winner has his jig featured on the cover of the book, with the second and third place winners featured on the back cover.

The criteria for judging the submissions included simplicity of design, ease of construction, use of inexpensive materials and versatility.

The first place winner is Jack Rich, who sent us the idea for the adjustable router base. Second place went to Guy Avery for the table saw fixture for cutting compound miters. Third place went to Harvey Freeman for the face-routing system for cabinet doors.

Nick Engler has several projects in this book and we thank him for his wonderfully creative ideas. Mary Jane Favorite, Nick's wife, created the technical illustrations for Nick's projects.

Photo credits go to Al Parrish who photographed Nick Engler's projects.

Thanks also go to *Popular Woodworking* magazine editors Chris Schwarz, David Thiel and Steve Shanesy for their kind permission to reprint many of the projects featured in this book.

Additional thanks go to Jim Stuard, Michel Theriault and Jack Bowley for their excellent projects.

Table of Contents

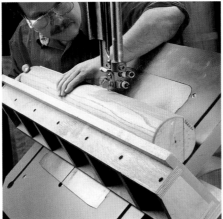

HAND TOOLS

DRILL PRESS

BAND SAW

MITER SAW

MISCELLANEOUS

Introduction

By definition, a jig guides your tool and a fixture guides your work. A table saw sled is a fixture because it guides the part that is being cut, and the adjustable router base shown on the cover of this book is a jig because it guides the router. However, the adjustable router base becomes a fixture when it is inverted and clamped to a sawhorse!

Hand and power woodworking tools are designed for specific tasks. However, sometimes these tools are asked to do things that they weren't originally intended to do. That's where the jigs and fixtures come into play. A table saw can be used as a jointer, and a drill press can cut mortises. We've also included a number of hand tools you can make from your scraps of wood and leftover hardware.

Most of us enjoy woodworking because it satisfies the creative side of our beings. We can create works with our hands, hearts and minds out of a material that still breathes and moves with the seasons long after it grew fruit or nuts, held climbers and swings and created shade.

Our hope is that this book will give you, the woodworker, some new and creative ideas for jigs and fixtures that will help you in your quest to create the works of wonder you see in your mind's eye.

We wish to thank all the woodworkers we've come in contact with over the years, because you've taught us a new trick or technique, given us encouragement when the joint wasn't perfect and rejoiced with us when the finish *did* come out perfect.

JIM STACK • EDITOR OF POPULAR WOODWORKING BOOKS

PROJECT

1

Compound Miter Fixture for the Table Saw

This fixture makes cutting compound miters child's play.

BY GUY AVERY

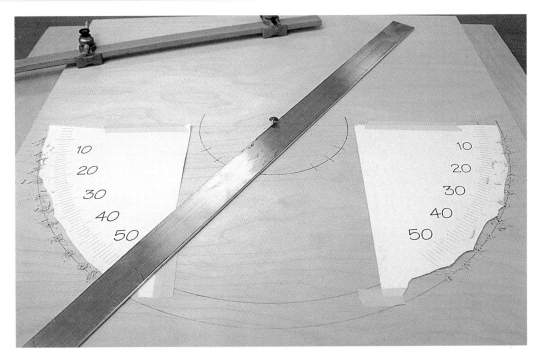

1 Put a brad or nail in the center of the base and use it to register the edge of a straightedge when drawing the degree marks on the sled. You can copy the degree marks illustrations to use as guides.

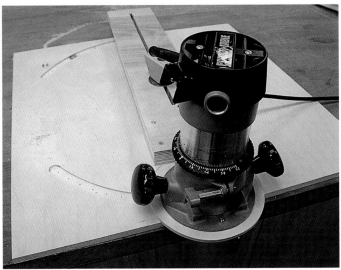

2 Rout a shallow groove to accept the heads of the T-nuts. If you drill the clearance holes for the T-nuts first, that will help you put this groove where it needs to be.

3 Hold the miter fences where they will be located on the sled and mark the curved slots. Then use the drill press to drill a series of holes. Clean out the slot and you're good to go.

This fixture will enable you to cut perfect compound miters every time.

Cut the parts as shown in the cutting list. Lay out the circles on the base as shown in the illustration. Put a small brad or nail in the center of the base and use this as a pivot point to register a straightedge. Hold the straightedge against the nail and draw the degree marks along the 20"-diameter circle (step 1). To help with this process, you might want to enlarge the degree illustrations to full size and use these as templates to lay out the degree marks. Then, drill clearance holes every 5° for the T-nut locations along the 22"-diameter line, as shown in the illustration.

Turn the base over and rout a shallow slot to accept the heads of the T-nuts, then install the T-nuts (step 2). Center the hardwood runner on the base and attach it with three No. 6 × ³⁄₄" wood screws. Finally, install the stiffener fence.

Lower the blade on your table saw and tilt it to 15° or 20°. Put the sled in one of the miter slots on the table saw top. Move the sled over the throat in the top to the approximate area where the saw blade slot in the sled will be located, as shown in the illustration. Turn on the saw, carefully raise the saw blade and cut the slot in the sled. Lower the blade, move the sled to the other miter slot in the table and cut the second slot in the sled.

Cut a 43° bevel on one end of each of the miter fences, mark the fences for the curved slots and cut them on the drill press (step 3). Make the knobs and drill for the carriage bolts, as shown in the drawing.

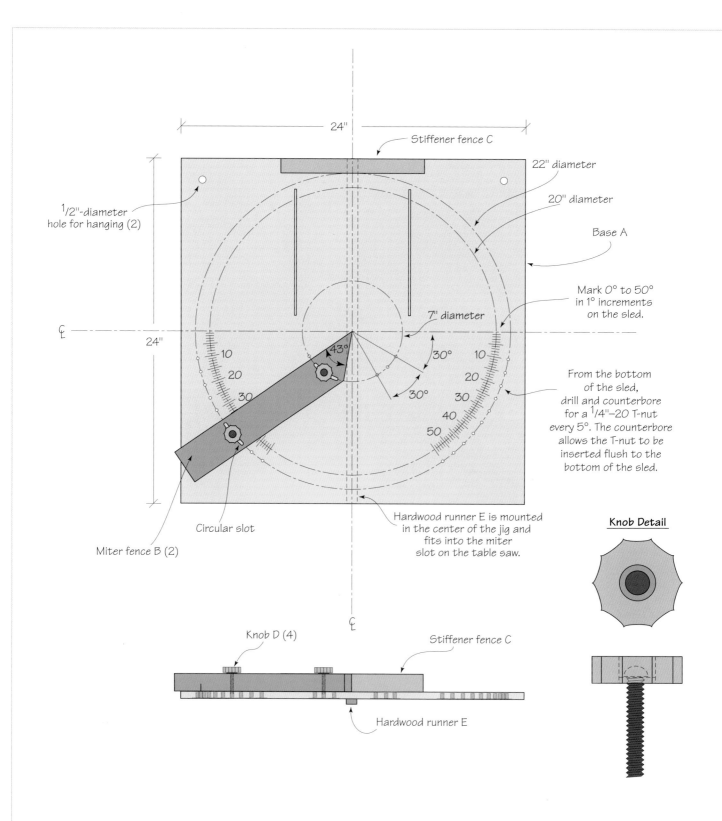

24"

Stiffener fence C

22" diameter

20" diameter

Base A

1/2"-diameter
hole for hanging (2)

Mark 0° to 50°
in 1° increments
on the sled.

7" diameter

30°

30°

43°

10

20

30

10

20

30

40

50

From the bottom
of the sled,
drill and counterbore
for a 1/4"–20 T-nut
every 5°. The counterbore
allows the T-nut to be
inserted flush to the
bottom of the sled.

24"

24"

Circular slot

Miter fence B (2)

Hardwood runner E is mounted
in the center of the jig and
fits into the miter
slot on the table saw.

Knob Detail

Knob D (4)

Stiffener fence C

Hardwood runner E

inches (millimeters)

REFERENCE	QUANTITY	PART	STOCK	THICKNESS	(mm)	WIDTH	(mm)	LENGTH	(mm)
A	1	base	plywood	1/2	(13)	24	(610)	24	(610)
B	2	miter fences	hardwood	1 1/4	(32)	2 1/2	(64)	15	(381)
C	1	stiffener fence	hardwood	1	(25)	1 1/4	(32)	10	(254)
D	4	knobs	plywood	3/4	(19)	2	(51)	2	(51)
E	1	hardwood runner	hardwood	3/8	(10)	3/4	(19)	24	(610)

HARDWARE

28 1/4"–20 (6mm–20) T-nuts

4 1/4" (6mm) fender washers

4 1 1/2" × 1/4"–20 (38mm × 6mm–20) carriage bolts

3 No. 6 × 3/4" wood screws

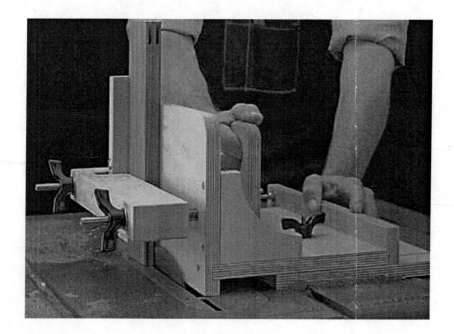

FORUM | **ASK A PRO** | **PROJECT ALBUM** | **CLUBS** | **CLASSIFIEDS** | **SUBSCRIBE** | **ARTICLES** | **WOODSHC**

FAQ   Search   Memberlist   Top posters   Album   Register   Profile   Private messages   Log in

I'm on a roll

newtopic   postreply   🖨   **Workshop Buzz Forum Index -> Workshop Buzz**

View prev

Author	Message

OldMan

Joined: 27 Apr 2004
Posts: 322
Location: Kingston, NS

🗋 Posted: Sat Mar 25, 2006 10:06 am   Post subject: I'm on a roll

With shop fixtures that is, after just recently completing my much needed router tabl
press table. My own design based on numerous photos I had seen on the web. I hav(
coming from LV for thin boards in addition to the horizontal clamp shown in the phot(
birch, plus all of the jig hardware from LV. Table size is 24" x 16" x 1"

I think this will allow me to have more efficient and repeatable results with my drill p
out there was putting off building such a jig, that these photos might motivate you! 1
x 1/2" sacrificial insert.

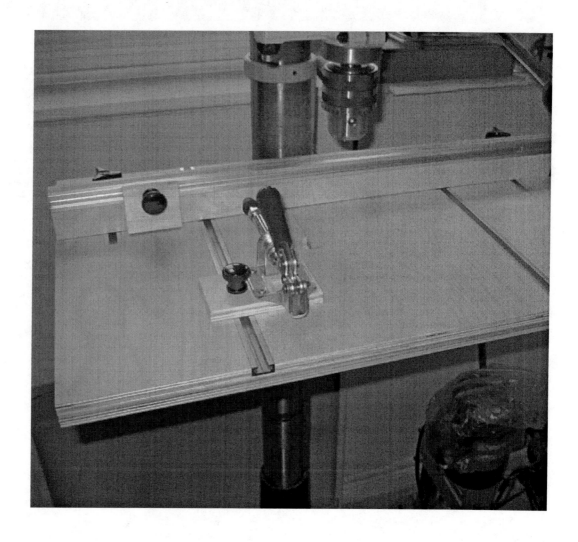

Back to top

acheyne

Joined: 21 Dec 2004
Posts: 87
Location: Bedford, Nova
Scotia

(profile) (pm)

□ Posted: Sat Mar 25, 2006 6:45 pm   Post subject:

Out of curiousity, what would you use a fence on a drill press for anyway?

Andrew

PS: Looks great, just have no idea what I'd use it for!

Back to top

Gary in Niagara

Joined: 01 Apr 2004
Posts: 54
Location: Fenwick, Ontario

(profile) (pm) (www)

□ Posted: Sat Mar 25, 2006 8:31 pm   Post subject:

> acheyne wrote:
> Out of curiousity, what would you use a fence on a drill press for anyway?

If you have a few holes to drill that all need to be 2 3/16" from the edge of a few pie
may come in handy. Now add in that stop and you can drill these holes the same dist

_____
Gary in Niagara (Fenwick, ON)

(profile) (pm) (email)

Back to top

OldMan

Joined: 27 Apr 2004
Posts: 322
Location: Kingston, NS

□ Posted: Sat Mar 25, 2006 8:46 pm   Post subject:

akabek,

sounds like you have the ideal setup for using the same fastening system I did. Befor
sheets together, place the bottom one on your metal DP table and trace on the unde
for a bolt to pass through. I drilled a total of four through holes in these locations. Th
accomodate one of these:

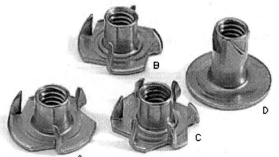

1/4-20 hardware shown.

I counterbored very slightly before hammering the hardware in, so that when the T-r
between the boards they wouldn't affect the flatness of the top.

Then all you need are some of these handles and washers to distribute the load unde
with the bolt portion hacksawed to the appropriate length.

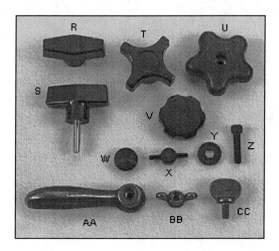

It seems to work well, plenty of clamping strength with no clamps or bolts getting in

_____

If trees could scream, would we still be cutting them down? We might, if they scream
reason.

Back to top

[profile] [pm]

busman

Joined: 21 May 2004
Posts: 929
Location: Kingston Ontario

Posted: Sun Mar 26, 2006 7:40 am   Post subject:

I like what you have done., I am going to change mine, to a similar design..I made c

I was going to make it like the incra table..yours is pretty close.

One question about the centre insert, that you can replace..Instead of having a 3/4 ∈
you need to replace it, isnt there going to be a hole in the centre from usage that yo

_____

A true friend is a person that knows all your faults and is still your friend.

Back to top

OldMan

Joined: 27 Apr 2004
Posts: 322
Location: Kingston, NS

Posted: Sun Mar 26, 2006 8:07 am   Post subject:

busman,

The holes in the plate after use may all be 1/8" it depends on what job you were doir
went a little large for the corner hole but I was in the mind set of using it for my fing
hole and use a screw driver to lift up the plate.

_____

If trees could scream, would we still be cutting them down? We might, if they scream
reason.

Back to top

busman

Joined: 21 May 2004
Posts: 929
Location: Kingston Ontario

Posted: Sun Mar 26, 2006 8:16 am   Post subject:

Old man i was just thinking it may be a place for wood chips to collect, unless you ha
Maybe being to picky , i really like the table..You did a great job and thought of ever
pretty cheesy looking.

My big mistake was i made the fence to high, and when i move the table up high, i h
handles on the drill press.
I have the track and hold down track , material, just need to take the time and do it

Thanks for posting and Picture..it will help alot..

Bus

_____

A true friend is a person that knows all your faults and is still your friend.

Back to top

Woody in the Hat   Posted: Mon Mar 27, 2006 1:12 pm   Post subject:

acheyne wrote:

Out of curiousity, what would you use a fence on a drill press for anyway?

Andrew

PS: Looks great, just have no idea what I'd use it for!

Joined: 01 Apr 2004
Posts: 1365
Location: Medicine Hat, Alberta

Gary pretty well covered it. But just to be more specific, I make small trinket boxes a occaisionally the Barrel Hinges for the lids. Drilling the holes for these hinges require: up like Oldman's makes the task a breeze.

Pin Hinge

Barrel & Roto Hinge

Regards,

Wendall / Woody in the Hat
Maintenance-free means when it breaks, it can't be fixed.

Back to top   (profile) (pm) (email) (www)

Display posts from previous: All Posts ▓ Oldest First ▓ Go

View prev

**Workshop Buzz Forum Index -> Workshop
Buzz**   All times are GMT - 5 Hours

Page 1 of 1

Jump to: Workshop Buzz ▓ Go

You **cannot** post new topics in this forum
You **cannot** reply to topics in this forum
You **cannot** edit your posts in this forum
You **cannot** delete your posts in this forum
You **cannot** vote in polls in this forum

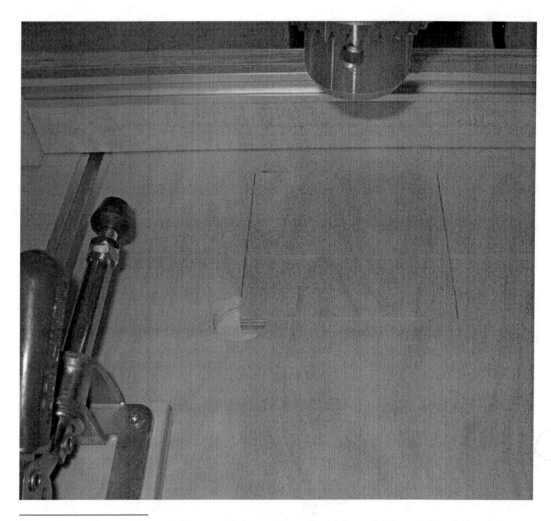

_____

If trees could scream, would we still be cutting them down? We might, if they scream reason.

[profile] [pm]

Richard in Smithville

Joined: 01 Apr 2004
Posts: 919
Location: Smithville,
Ontario

□ Posted: Sat Mar 25, 2006 10:14 am   Post subject:

Looks good. Certainly beats the 12x18 bit of 3/4 ply bolted to my dp table.

Richard To know the road ahead, ask those coming back

[profile] [pm]

Hickory

□ Posted: Sat Mar 25, 2006 10:56 am   Post subject:

For an old man you come on strong.... That is the best looking design for a Drill Pres ones in the Design Mags., etc. are either too complicated or big and ugly. I like yours it to a mag. before someone around here beat you to it.

Joined: 04 Apr 2004
Posts: 2755
Location: Kentucky

Back to top

(There are elements around here that steal designs and claim them as their trophys,

In fact I suggest you pull your pictures till you get it submitted.
_____

Men don't plan to fail, they often fail to plan.
If you don't learn something new every day, you're not paying attention...

---

jimbo268

Joined: 06 Dec 2005
Posts: 6
Location: Sarnia, Ontario

Back to top

Posted: Sat Mar 25, 2006 2:12 pm   Post subject: Drill press table

Your table looks great, I've been thinking of making one my self. Question? Your cut
insert to make your table a oscillating sander as well? 😊 Jim H.

OldMan

Joined: 27 Apr 2004
Posts: 322
Location: Kingston, NS

Back to top

Posted: Sat Mar 25, 2006 3:07 pm   Post subject:

Hickory, thanks for the comments. No worries about anyone stealing my design as it
I had seen photos of. But if you do see it in a magazine, just remember you saw it h

jimbo, the square cutout acts as a backer board to prevent blowout when drilling. On
slip in a new 4" x 4" piece of baltic birch. I suppose that space could be used with a
1/2" is enough clearance for the bottom of the drums.
_____

If trees could scream, would we still be cutting them down? We might, if they scream
reason.

---

akabek

Joined: 27 Oct 2004
Posts: 113
Location: Newmarket, ON

Back to top

Posted: Sat Mar 25, 2006 6:08 pm   Post subject:

Excellent job on the table. I am in the processes of making one myself of a similar de
alumuminum extrusion off of ebay for the fence. While at home depot today I purcha
melamine off cuts for a $1 each. They are 1/2" each and I was planning to glue them
the table to the drill press? I was thinking of installing a couple of screw inserts at th
hold down clamps. Great job

Ryan in Penetang

Joined: 27 Mar 2005
Posts: 280
Location: Penetanguishene,
ON

Posted: Sat Mar 25, 2006 6:17 pm   Post subject:

Don't worry about it Hickory...I have the EXACT same table! Mines MDF, and the alu
apart from that.....the same! Even the dimensions are within 1/2 inch. LOL......I built
_____

If you can't set a good example.....at least serve as a horrible warning!

Check out my website:
www.rarewoodcreations.com

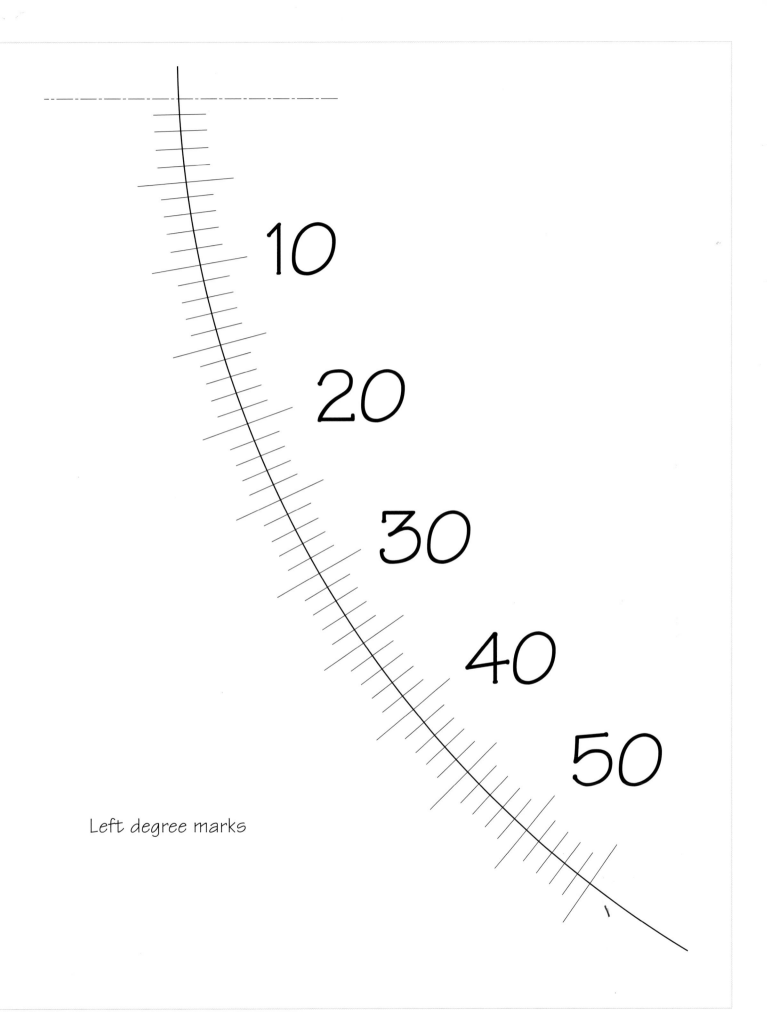

10

20

30

40

50

Left degree marks

10

20

30

40

50

Right degree marks

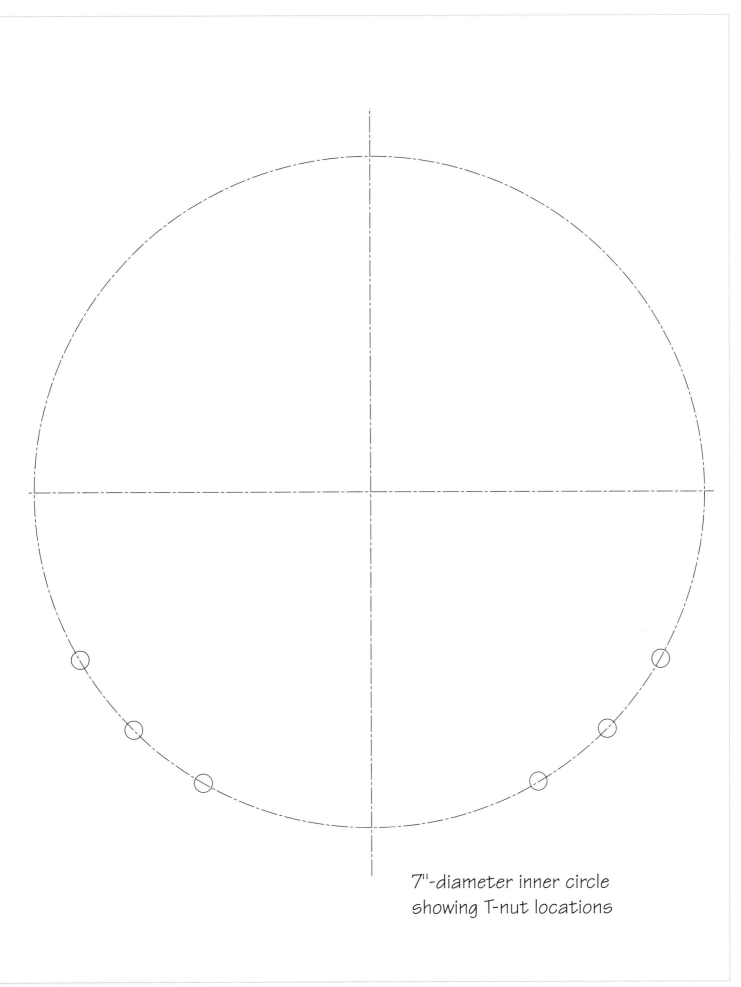

7"-diameter inner circle
showing T-nut locations

COMPOUND MITER CHART FOR THE TABLE SAW

Slope	4 sides butted Miter ang	Bevel ang	4 sides mitered Miter ang	Bevel ang	5 sides mitered Miter ang	Bevel ang	6 sides mitered Miter ang	Bevel ang	8 sides mitered Miter ang	Bevel ang
0			45	90	54	90	60	90	67.5	90
5			45.11	3.53	54.1	2.94	60.09	2.5	67.58	1.91
10			45.44	7.05	54.42	5.86	60.38	4.98	67.81	3.81
15			45.99	10.55	54.94	8.75	60.85	7.44	68.19	5.69
20			46.78	14	55.68	11.6	61.52	9.85	68.73	7.52
25			47.81	17.39	56.64	14.38	62.38	12.2	69.42	9.31
30	49.11	48.59	49.11	20.7	57.82	17.09	63.43	14.48	70.27	11.03
35	50.68	42.14	50.68	23.93	59.24	19.7	64.69	16.67	71.26	12.68
40	52.55	35.93	52.55	27.03	60.9	22.2	66.14	18.75	72.4	14.24
45	54.74	30	54.74	30	62.81	24.56	67.79	20.71	73.68	15.7
50	57.27	24.4	57.27	32.8	64.97	26.76	69.64	22.52	75.09	17.05
55	60.16	19.21	60.16	35.4	67.38	28.78	71.68	24.18	76.64	18.26
60	63.43	14.48	63.43	37.77	70.04	30.59	73.9	25.66	78.3	19.35
65	67.09	10.29	67.09	39.86	72.93	32.19	76.29	26.94	80.07	20.29
70	71.12	6.72	71.12	41.64	76.05	33.52	78.83	28.02	81.94	21.07
75	75.49	3.84	75.49	43.08	79.35	34.59	81.5	28.88	83.88	21.7
80	80.15	1.73	80.15	44.13	82.81	35.37	84.27	29.52	85.89	22.12
85	85.02	0.44	85.02	44.78	86.38	35.82	87.12	29.87	87.93	22.43
90	90	0	90	45	90	36	90	30	90	22.5

Slope	10 sides mitered Miter ang	Bevel ang	12 sides mitered Miter ang	Bevel ang	16 sides mitered Miter ang	Bevel ang	20 sides mitered Miter ang	Bevel ang	24 sides mitered Miter ang	Bevel ang
0	72	90	75	90	78.75	90	81	90	82.5	90
5	72.06	1.54	75.05	1.29	78.79	0.97	81.03	0.78	82.53	0.65
10	72.26	3.08	75.22	2.58	78.92	1.94	81.13	1.56	82.61	1.3
15	72.58	4.59	75.49	3.84	79.12	2.9	81.3	2.32	82.75	1.94
20	73.02	6.07	75.87	5.08	79.41	3.83	81.53	3.07	82.95	2.56
25	73.59	7.5	76.35	6.28	79.78	4.73	81.83	3.79	83.2	3.16
30	74.28	8.89	76.94	7.43	80.23	5.6	82.19	4.49	83.5	3.74
35	75.1	10.21	77.62	8.54	80.75	6.42	82.61	5.15	83.84	4.3
40	76.02	11.46	78.4	9.58	81.34	7.2	83.08	5.77	84.24	4.81
45	77.06	12.62	79.27	10.55	81.99	7.93	83.61	6.35	84.68	5.3
50	78.2	13.7	80.23	11.43	82.71	8.6	84.19	6.88	85.16	5.74
55	79.44	14.67	81.26	12.24	83.49	9.2	84.81	7.36	85.68	6.14
60	80.77	15.53	82.37	12.95	84.32	9.73	85.47	7.79	86.23	6.5
65	82.18	16.27	83.54	13.56	85.19	10.19	86.17	8.15	86.82	6.78
70	83.66	16.88	84.76	14.09	86.11	10.56	86.9	8.45	87.42	7.05
75	85.19	17.38	86.03	14.49	87.05	10.87	87.65	8.7	88.05	7.24
80	86.77	17.72	87.34	14.75	88.02	11.09	88.42	8.89	88.69	7.39
85	88.38	17.91	88.66	14.97	89.01	11.17	89.21	8.96	89.34	7.5
90	90	18	90	15	90	11.25	90	9	90	45

NOTE: The slope is measured from horizontal, with the assembly resting on a bench or work surface.

Dovetail Fixture for the Table Saw

This dovetail fixture isn't for the birds. It really works.

BY JIM STACK

The table saw is a great tool to use to cut dovetails. You can create the look of hand-cut dovetails and take advantage of what the table saw does well — cutting straight and square.

To make the fixture, first cut the parts as shown in the materials list. Then attach the miter guide to the bottom center of the base, using three No. 6 × ¾" wood screws.

Attach the mounting cleats to their respective fences. Then attach the long fence assembly to the base, using one No. 8 × 1½" wood screw at the end of the mounting cleat. Put the base on the table saw with the miter guide in either of the two miter slots in the top of the saw. Locate where the saw blade will be cutting into the sled. Mount a blade guard block on the back of the fence assembly, then move the sled so the miter guide is in the other slot in the table saw top. Mark and mount another blade guard block where the blade will cut into the sled.

Unplug the saw and raise the table saw blade to its full height. Keep the sled in one of the slots on the tabletop. Lay a framing square on the top of the sled and rest one arm of the square against the fence. Let the other arm of the square stick out toward the saw blade. Align the edge of this arm along the side of the saw blade and move the

fence until it is square to the saw blade. Put another screw at the other end of the fence mounting cleat.

Cut a 10° angle on the left end of one of the angled fences and on the right end of the other fence. You can do this on the table saw. Use a miter

gauge set to 80° to the left and make the cut on one fence. Set the miter gauge 80° to the right and cut the opposite end of the other angled fence.

Turn the sled around 180° and put the miter guide in the tabletop slot to the left of the saw blade. Put the

I usually cut the pins of the dovetails first, but it's just fine to cut the tails first if you like. Try it both ways and see which works best for you. Start by laying out the dovetails on your stock, spacing them to your personal tastes. Cut one edge of the pins freehand, using the sled to cut to your marks. Move the sled to the other tabletop slot, move the stock to the other fence and cut the other side of the pins. Nibble the waste between the pins by moving the stock a little at a time across the saw blade. If there is any variation in the pins, or if they aren't exactly the same width, don't worry. You're going to use these pins as a template to lay out the tails on the other parts. Be sure to mark each end with its mate.

right-hand angled fence on the sled as shown in the illustration. Using a sliding T-bevel set to 10°, and holding the bevel against the side of the saw blade, attach the fence to the sled. Move the sled to the slot to the right of the saw blade and attach the other fence in the same manner.

Mark where the saw blade will cut into the sled on each of the angled fences and attach the remaining two blade guard blocks, one on each fence.

Plug in the saw and make test-cuts to double-check all the angles. Make adjustments if necessary.

Apply paste wax to the bottom of the slide and miter-guide strip. This will allow the sled to slide easily on the table saw top.

After marking the tails using the pins as your template, set the table saw blade at a 10° angle and cut the cheeks of the tails. Cut the left cheek, flip the stock face for face and cut the right cheek. Then, set the saw blade back to vertical and cut as much of the waste as you can between the tails. You can clean up the inside corners of the cutout with a chisel. If you plan to cut a lot of dovetails and want to make this process go even smoother, have all the teeth on a saw blade ground to a 10° angle so that the tilted saw blade will cut the corners cleanly between the tails. Be sure to double-check the tilt of your saw blade so you can tell your saw sharpener which way to grind the 10° angle!

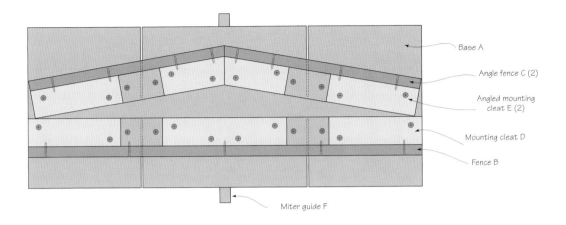

Base A

Angle fence C (2)

Angled mounting cleat E (2)

Mounting cleat D

Fence B

Miter guide F

Blade guard block G (4)

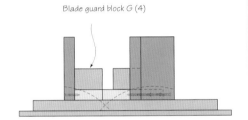

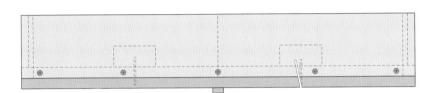

inches (millimeters)

REFERENCE	QUANTITY	PART	STOCK	THICKNESS	(mm)	WIDTH	(mm)	LENGTH	(mm)
A	1	base	plywood	3/4	(19)	11 1/2	(292)	28	(711)
B	1	fence	plywood	3/4	(19)	4 1/2	(114)	28	(711)
C	2	angled fences	plywood	3/4	(19)	4 1/2	(114)	14	(356)
D	1	mounting cleat	plywood	3/4	(19)	2	(51)	28	(711)
E	2	angled mounting cleats	plywood	3/4	(19)	2	(51)	14	(356)
F	1	miter guide	hardwood	3/8	(10)	3/4	(19)	13 1/2	(343)
G	4	blade guard blocks	hardwood	1 1/2	(38)	2	(51)	3	(76)

HARDWARE

29   No. 8 × 1 1/2" (No. 8 × 38mm) flathead wood screws

3   No. 6 × 3/4" (No. 6 × 19mm) flathead wood screws

TABLE SAW

Jointer for the Table Saw

Straighten things up with this simple, two-board jig.

BY JIM STACK

Many of us don't own jointers. But that doesn't mean we can't make a straight edge on a board. This simple little jig will create straight edges on hardwood, softwood and plywood.

The amount of material that is removed from the board being straightened is determined by the thickness of the outfeed spacer. It is recommended that no more that $3/32$" be removed at one time. That's a little more than half the thickness of a standard carbide-tipped saw blade.

To use the jig, attach it to the saw's fence. Lower the saw blade and move the jig slightly over the top of the saw blade. Turn on the saw, raise the blade and cut into the jig about 1" or so. Make test-cuts until the amount of material removed equals the thickness of the outfeed spacer.

For repeated usage, make a note on the jig as to what saw blade you used and the setting on the fence's hairline ruler gauge.

1 Cut the parts and glue the outfeed spacer to the fence. If the fence is bent, glue the spacer to the concave side of the fence.

2 If the fence is bent and you've glued the spacer to the concave side, when you put a clamp at each end of the jig, the middle will pull tightly to the saw's fence. Be sure the stock will clear the clamps.

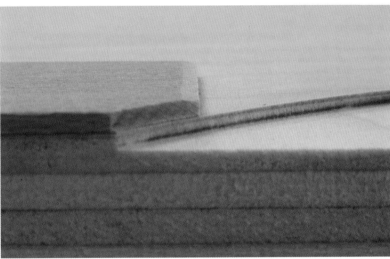

3 Cut a small bevel on the leading edge of the outfeed spacer to ease the feed of the wood against the jig.

inches (millimeters)

REFERENCE	QUANTITY	PART	STOCK	THICKNESS	(mm)	WIDTH	(mm)	LENGTH	(mm)
A	1	fence	plywood	3/4	(19)	4	(102)	36	(914)
B	1	outfeed spacer	hardwood	1/16	(2)	1	(25)	10	(254)

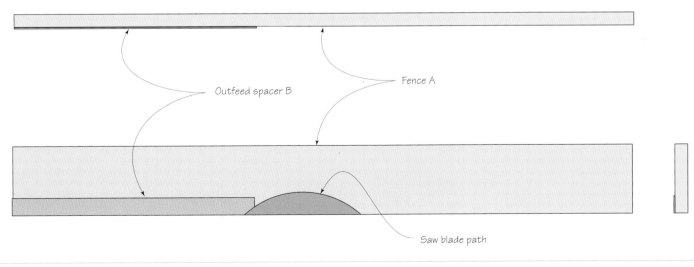

Outfeed spacer B

Fence A

Saw blade path

TABLE SAW

Microadjustable Finger-Joint Jig

What a difference a machine screw makes.

BY NICK ENGLER

You find them lurking in bins in hardware stores, hanging out in plastic bags in home centers, rusting in baby food jars in garages and basements all across America: flathead machine screws with 32 threads per inch. Few of us ever suspect that these unpretentious bits of hardware could be so incredibly helpful, particularly to those of us who still use the ancient and venerable English system of measurements. These tiny machine screws are a cure for many troubles that afflict our accuracy. They can eliminate the error from a trial-and-error method and turn a homemade jig into precision equipment.

Consider the traditional finger-joint jig. It's designed to make evenly spaced square notches in the ends of adjoining boards, leaving multiple tenons that interlock to form a finger joint. The standard finger-joint jig has just three parts: a back that you attach to your miter gauge, a movable face that feeds the wood into a dado blade to cut the notches, and a tenon that aligns the wood for each cut. To set up this jig, you must move the face right or left, adjusting the space between the tenon and the dado blade, so the fingers will be properly spaced. If the fingers are too close together, the joint will be loose. Too far apart and they will be too tight to assemble easily.

Positioning the face properly is often a frustrating loop of trials and errors. Cut a finger joint, test the fit, move the face, cut another joint and so on. But if you add one more part to this jig — a small wooden block that mounts a No. 10–32 machine screw and serves as an adjustable stop — you can escape this frustration.

Because the machine screw has 32 threads per inch, one turn will move it precisely $\frac{1}{32}$"; one-half turn moves it $\frac{1}{64}$"; one-quarter turn, $\frac{1}{128}$". When the flat head is resting against the face, the face will move a precise amount. No guesswork!

When constructing this finger-joint jig, remember that the tenon must be precisely the same width as the fingers you wish to cut. I made several faces for my jig, each with different-size tenons.

Make the tenon and stop from hardwood such as oak or maple. Drill a $\frac{5}{32}$"-diameter hole for the machine screw, then cut threads in the hole with a tap. (You can purchase a No. 10–32 tap at most hardware stores.) Oak and maple are hard enough to hold the fine threads, but soft enough that they spring back and hold the machine screw in position. To make it easier to turn the machine screw, install a knurled nut on the end and tighten a stop nut against it.

These stops have many other applications besides finger joints. I use them as fence stops on my router table and drill press. I've incorporated them in cutoff boxes, tenoning fixtures and other applications where a small adjustment can make the difference between good craftsmanship and great craftsmanship.

Tip: To keep the dado blade from splintering the wood where it exits the cuts, scribe the length of the fingers on the board. Make the fingers about $\frac{1}{32}$" longer than the width of the board so they protrude slightly when you assemble them. Later you can sand the ends and faces flush.

Making a Finger Joint

1 Initially, set up the finger-joint jig by making a few rough measurements with a ruler. The tenon, the dado blade and the distance between them should all be the same width, in this case, $\frac{1}{4}$".

2 Make a test-cut. Butt the edge of the board against the tenon and feed the wood forward, cutting a notch. The resulting tenon should be exactly $\frac{1}{4}$" wide.

3 To cut multiple fingers, move the board sideways, fit the notch over the tenon and cut again. Continue until you have cut all the fingers. Note that the last finger on this trial board is not as thick as the others.

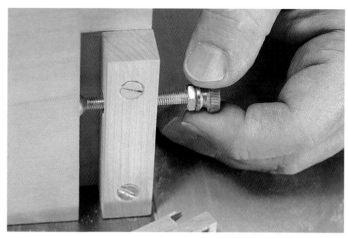

4 Since the board is 4" wide and the fingers are supposed to be $1/4$" wide, the fingers should have come out evenly. Checking with a micrometer, I find they are $1/64$" too narrow: The tenon needs to be $1/64$" further away from the dado blade. I loosen the face and turn the machine screw one-half turn.

5 When the jig is properly adjusted, it's time to cut the good stuff. Make a single finger in one of the adjoining boards as you did in the second step. Turn the board edge for edge and fit the notch over the tenon. Use the first board as a spacer to make the initial cut in the second board.

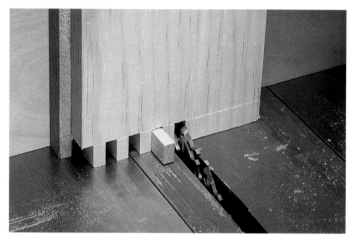

6 Place the notches in the boards over the tenon and cut more notches. Continue, cutting both adjoining boards at once. Note: If the fingers are spaced properly and the joint is still too tight or too loose, adjust the width of the dado blade. I invested in a set of thin brass dado shims just for this purpose.

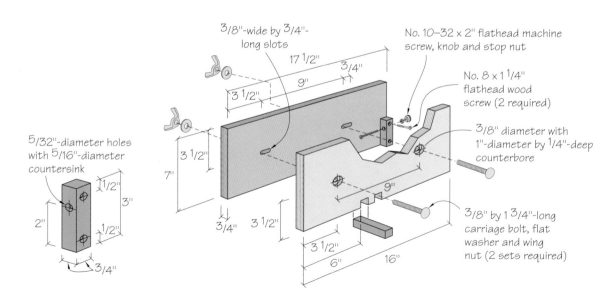

$3/8$"-wide by $3/4$"-long slots

No. 10–32 x 2" flathead machine screw, knob and stop nut

$17 1/2$"

$3/4$"

9"

No. 8 x 1 $1/4$" flathead wood screw (2 required)

$3 1/2$"

$3/8$" diameter with 1"-diameter by $1/4$"-deep counterbore

$5/32$"-diameter holes with $5/16$"-diameter countersink

$1/2$"

3"

$3 1/2$"

7"

2"

$1/2$"

9"

$3/4$"

$3 1/2$"

$3/4$"

$3/8$" by 1 $3/4$"-long carriage bolt, flat washer and wing nut (2 sets required)

$3 1/2$"

6"

16"

Multipurpose Saw Sled

It takes just nine pieces of wood to turn your table saw into a precision crosscutting and tenoning machine.

BY NICK ENGLER

For many years I had the pleasure of working with Jim McCann, a craftsman I admired as much for his ingenuity as his considerable skill. Jim and I designed projects of all sorts, but we had a special fondness for jigs. It was a challenge for us to create a shop-made tool as simple and as functional as possible. This sliding table or saw sled was one of our best efforts. There are really four jigs here — the sliding table itself, an auxiliary table to prevent binding and kickbacks, a microadjustable fence stop for duplication and accuracy and a tenoning jig to hold stock vertically — just nine wooden parts to do dozens of sawing chores.

Sliding Table

The table is a large base with a long fence that slides across the saw table, past the saw blade. A miter bar attached to the underside of the base guides the jig. This is the one special piece of hardware you need to make this jig — a miter bar to fit the slot in your particular table saw. (Most are ³/₈" deep and ³/₄" wide.) Use medium-density fiberboard (MDF) for the base, and attach the bar to the base with machine screws, countersinking the heads so they're slightly below the surface of the base. Position the bar so that when you saw

with the jig for the first time, the blade shaves about 1/16" from the edge of the sled's base.

Make the fence from a single piece of straight-grained hardwood. Tip: To make a long, slender part such as the fence as stable as possible, rip it in half parallel to the annual rings. Rotate one part 180° and glue the parts back together so the annual rings cup in the opposite directions. This will help the fence stay straight and true.

Rip the board for your fence down the middle, joint both halves straight and cut two grooves in each half — a 3/4"-wide by 3/8"-deep groove followed by a 1/4"-wide groove all the way through the stock, as shown in the Elevation Section A drawing and the shaded area of the Fence Detail drawing. The grooves in the front half should run almost the complete length of the fence, while the grooves in the back half need to be only a few inches long. When you glue the fence halves back together, the grooves will form T-slots. Use the long T-slot on the front of the fence to mount the fence stop and the tenoning jig. The shorter slot on the back stores the stop and keeps it handy.

Mount the fence to the base with 3/8"

In addition to everything else it does, the sliding table also makes an excellent base for other sawing jigs that you might need. Here I've attached a special fence and clamps to make scarf joints in the spars for a reproduction of a Wright brothers' flyer.

Tip: To adjust the fence so it holds the wood precisely square to the saw blade, take a scrap piece and rip it so the edges are parallel. Mark one face, saw through the mark (left) and flip one part over. Bring the cut ends together, holding the edges against the fence (right). If the seam between the parts gaps at the top or bottom, the fence is not square to the blade.

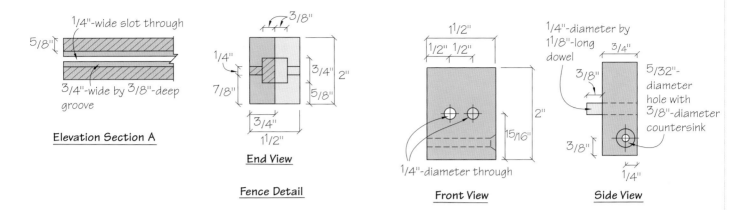

Elevation Section A

1/4"-wide slot through
5/8"
3/4"-wide by 3/8"-deep groove

Fence Detail

End View

3/8"
1/4"
7/8"
3/4"
1½"
3/4"
5/8"
2"

Front View

1½"
1/2" 1/2"
15/16"
2"
1/4"-diameter through

Side View

1/4"-diameter by 1¹/8"-long dowel
3/8"
3/4"
5/32"-diameter hole with 3/8"-diameter countersink
3/8"
1/4"

Use the tenoning jig and the fence stop in combination. Slide the tenoning jig into the T-slot, then slide the fence stop right behind it. Turn the microadjustment screw until it's snug against the end of the jig. Clamp a piece of wood in the cradle, make a test-cut and check the results. If you need to adjust the position of the jig, loosen the carriage bolts and rotate the adjustment screw. In this manner you can make very fine adjustments, getting the cut just right.

hex bolts. Drill counterbores for the heads of the bolts so they don't protrude from the underside of the base. The bolt nearest the saw blade serves as a pivot, should you need to angle the fence to cut miters. The other bolt secures the fence and provides a small amount of angle adjustment. The shank hole for this bolt is $^7/_{16}$" in diameter. That extra clearance lets you move the fence back and forth a few degrees to adjust it square to the blade. Once the fence is adjusted, draw a pencil line to mark the position of the fence on the base. If you ever need to change the

angle of the fence, the pencil line will make it easy to square it up again.

Since 95 percent of your saw cuts are made at 90°, and another $4^1/_2$ percent are made at 45°, I suggest you drill holes and counterbores so you can secure the fence at 90° and 45°, and leave it at that. For any odd angles, you can either drill holes as you need them or resort to your miter gauge.

To help measure as I cut, I added a scale to the front of the fence, inset in a $^1/_{32}$"-deep rabbet. Note that the scale is upside down. It's easier to read when I lean over the fence.

Auxiliary Table

One of the few drawbacks to a sliding table is that the base raises the work off the saw table, leaving it unsupported on the far side of the saw blade. Because of this, the wood will drop down as you finish the cut, binding the blade. This in turn may cause the cutoff part to kick back.

The auxiliary table (shown in the opening photo) prevents this. It's a second base the same size as the first, but without a fence or a miter bar. Instead, a cleat at the front edge hooks over your saw table and prevents the auxiliary

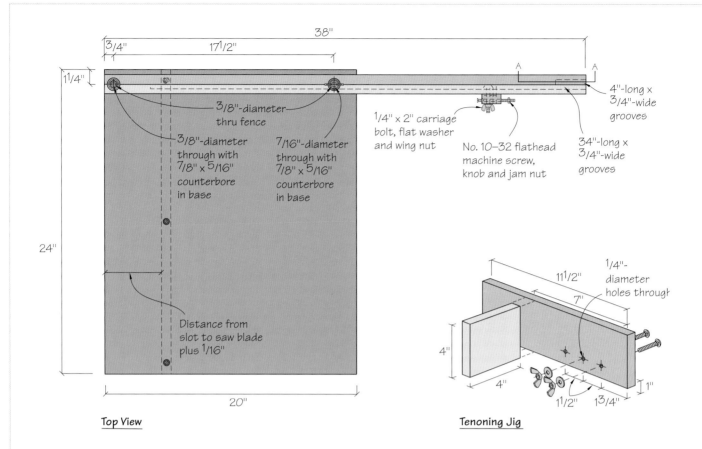

38"

3/4" 17 1/2"

1 1/4"

3/8"-diameter thru fence

3/8"-diameter through with 7/8" x 5/16" counterbore in base

7/16"-diameter through with 7/8" x 5/16" counterbore in base

1/4" x 2" carriage bolt, flat washer and wing nut

No. 10–32 flathead machine screw, knob and jam nut

4"-long x 3/4"-wide grooves

34"-long x 3/4"-wide grooves

A   A

24"

Distance from slot to saw blade plus 1/16"

20"

Top View

1/4"-diameter holes through

11 1/2"

7"

4"

4"

1 1/2" 1 3/4"

1"

Tenoning Jig

table from sliding forward as you work. Depending on the design of your saw, cut the cleat so that you can secure it with a clamp either to the fence rail or the front of the saw.

Fence Stop

The stop is a block of wood you can mount anywhere along the length of the fence to make duplicate cuts without having to measure for each cut. A 1/4" carriage bolt secures the stop in the T-slot, and a 1/4"-diameter dowel prevents it from pivoting. To get the stop to slide smoothly, you'll need to do a little file work. The head of a carriage bolt is stamped so there is a curved transition, or fillet, between the head and the square section at the beginning of the shaft. This fillet wedges itself in the slot and makes it difficult to move the stop. To fix this, file the carriage bolt to re-move the fillet, creating a square shoul-der between the head and the shank of the carriage bolt.

I also added a microadjustment to my stop. Drill a 5/32"-diameter hole through

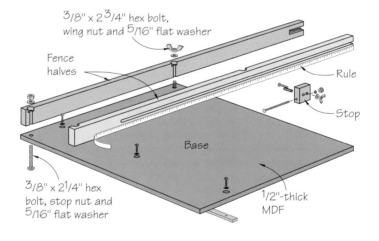

3/8" x 2 3/4" hex bolt, wing nut and 5/16" flat washer

Fence halves

Rule

Stop

3/8" x 2 1/4" hex bolt, stop nut and 5/16" flat washer

Base

1/2"-thick MDF

the stop and parallel to the bottom edge and thread this hole with a No. 10–32 tap. (A dense hardwood such as hard maple will take these small threads with no problem.) Countersink the end of the hole nearest the blade (when the stop is mounted to the fence). Turn a No. 10–32 flathead machine screw into the threaded hole and tighten a jam nut and a knurled nut on the other end so you can turn the screw easily. One turn of the screw will advance the head pre-cisely 1/32", allowing you to make ex-tremely accurate adjustments.

Tenoning Jig

The tenoning jig is two pieces of wood joined at 90°. This makes a cradle to hold boards vertically to the saw blade. Just place the board in the corner formed by the two parts and secure it with a clamp. Don't waste good wood on this jig; make it from scraps. The tenoning jig is a "disposable" fixture. It eventually gets eaten up by the saw blade, and you'll have to make a new one. Mount the jig to the fence with two 1/4" carriage bolts, much the same way you mounted the fence stop.

Panel-Cutting Sled

Here's a slick little sled that gives a square cut every time.

BY CHRIS SCHWARZ

We recently moved our shop to a smaller location and had to get rid of several tools. One of the first casualties was a gargantuan sliding crosscut table attached to our table saw. Though it's a useful accessory, it has some serious drawbacks. Namely, it takes up more than its fair share of space and needs to be recalibrated every time you attach it to the saw.

We already own a few nice jigs for crosscutting narrow stock, but for cutting wide panels — tabletops, cabinet sides and shelves, for example — we needed to come up with another solution.

This jig is just the ticket. It can easily handle panels as large as 24" wide and 36" long, which should cover 99 percent of your crosscutting needs. It has a couple of other useful features you don't find on most people's sleds: First, you can square it to the blade and recalibrate it when necessary (such as when you drop the jig or your saw's settings change). Most sleds don't have this feature and need to be trashed when they eventually become inaccurate.

Second, a replaceable zero-clearance face on the jig's fence makes cutting to a line a snap. All you do is mark directly on your work where you want to make your cut. Then you line up that line

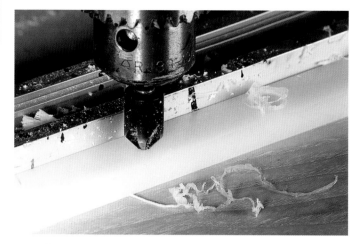

Use a fence on your drill press's table when drilling the holes and countersinks in the miter bar. Though I'm sure some of us could freehand this operation, a fence ensures your success.

If you followed the instructions carefully, you should trim only ⅛" off the sled base during its first pass on your table saw.

The number of screws looks like overkill, but they help prevent the bar from flexing and they allow you to take out any side-to-side play in the plastic bar by tightening the screws slightly.

with the edge of your zero-clearance fence face and make the cut.

Third, we've added a couple of tricks to that replaceable fence face that will help hold your work in place as you make your crosscut. The fence face is covered in adhesive-backed sandpaper,

plus a couple of nail points stick out ¹⁄₃₂" from the fence to grip your work. Don't get too worried about the freckle-size dimples left by these nails. If you're crosscutting plywood (a common chore), the holes will be covered by your edge tape or banding. If you're using solid wood, you can simply plane or sand the holes away, or make sure they end up on the back edge of your cabinet sides.

Finally, this jig is quick and cheap to make. We spent $22 on wood and hardware. (And with the exception of the miter bar, we had enough stuff left over to build a second sled.) Construction time was three hours flat.

Why MDF?

It's tempting to use birch plywood for the sled's base, but I don't recommend it. We've built quite a few sleds, and some of the plywood ones have warped and become unusable after a year or two of use. The plywood jigs that have survived well have been ones that are extrathick or have supplemental bracing to keep them flat.

Medium-density fiberboard (MDF) is inexpensive, easy to work and stable (as long as you don't take it for a swim).

Begin by cutting your sled base to size, then mark the line on the underside for attaching the miter bar. First, measure the distance between your saw blade and your miter slot. Add ½" to that measurement and mark that line on the underside of your sled. Now drill ³⁄₃₂" pilot holes on that line, using your drill press. Make your first hole 1" from the end and then every 2" afterwards.

Now drill corresponding ⅛" clear-

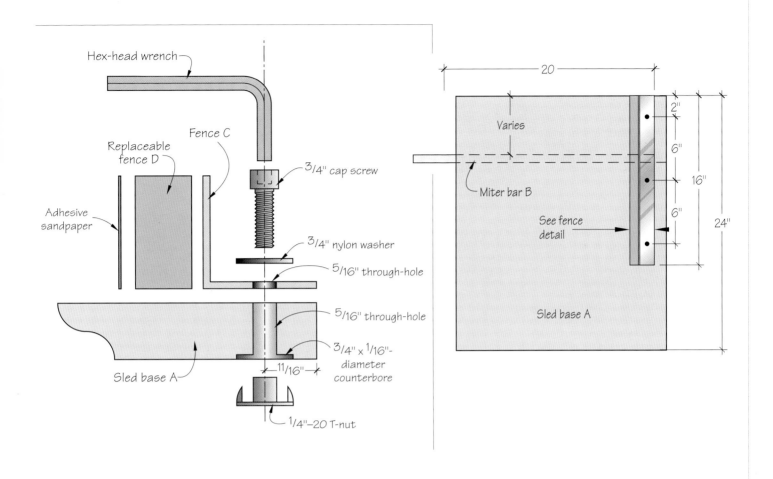

Hex-head wrench

Fence C

Replaceable fence D

Adhesive sandpaper

3/4" cap screw

3/4" nylon washer

5/16" through-hole

5/16" through-hole

3/4" × 1/16"-diameter counterbore

Sled base A

11/16"

1/4"–20 T-nut

20

Varies

Miter bar B

See fence detail

Sled base A

2"

6"

6"

16"

24"

inches (millimeters)

REFERENCE	QUANTITY	PART	STOCK	THICKNESS	(mm)	WIDTH	(mm)	LENGTH	(mm)
A	1	sled base	MDF	3/4	(19)	20	(508)	24	(610)
B	1	miter bar	UHMW	3/8	(10)	3/4	(19)	24	(610)
C	1	fence	aluminum	1 1/2	(38)	1 1/2	(38)	16	(406)
D	1	replaceable fence	plywood	3/4	(19)	1 1/2	(38)	16	(406)

HARDWARE

3/8" × 3/4" × 24" (10mm × 19mm × 610mm) UHMW miter bar	item #46J90.15	Lee Valley
1/4"–20 (6mm–20) T-nuts, 3-prong	item #00N22.03	Lee Valley
3/4" (19mm) cap screws	item #00M40.11	Lee Valley
1/4" (6mm) nylon washers	item #00M40.23	Lee Valley
1/8" × 1 1/2" × 36" (3mm × 38mm × 914mm) aluminum angle	found at any home-improvement store	
MDF	found at any home-improvement store	
No. 8 × 1" screws	found at any home-improvement store	

ance holes and countersinks in the miter bar. Why so many screws? Two reasons: One, you don't want any flex in your miter bar. And two, the screws compress the ultra-high molecular weight (UHMW) plastic bar slightly. This allows you to remove some slack in the miter bar when it is in your table saw's miter slot. Tighten a few screws for a tighter fit; loosen a few for a sloppier experience.

Screw the miter bar to your base, using No. 8 × 1" screws. Put the jig in place on your saw, raise the blade and trim the left edge of the sled to a perfect fit.

Precision Drilling

Next, you want to install the T-nuts that will hold the fence in place. T-nuts have a barrel that requires a 5/16" hole and a flange that needs a 1/16"-deep by 3/4"-diameter hole. Begin by drilling the 3/4" stopped hole in the locations shown in

T-nuts are easy to install using a hammer if you drilled your holes correctly in your base. Drill the ³⁄₄"-diameter hole for the flange, using a Forstner bit. Then use the hole left by the bit's spur to center the ⁵⁄₁₆" bit for the through-hole.

Here's the best way to square this jig. Hold the square's handle against the edge of the sled's base. Push the blade of the square against your fence and tighten the cap screws down against the nylon washers.

the diagram, using your drill press. Now chuck a ⁵⁄₁₆" bit into your drill press and drill the three through-holes you need. Tap the T-nuts in with a hammer.

Easy Metalworking

Now you need to drill some corresponding holes in the aluminum fence. If you've never drilled in aluminum, you'll find it a lot easier than you expected (especially if you've ever drilled steel).

The holes in the fence are also ⁵⁄₁₆" in diameter. This is a bit larger than the ¹⁄₄" shank on the cap screws, but it's this little bit of play that will allow you to square this jig to your saw blade.

Once those holes are drilled, drill a few ¹⁄₈" holes in the other wing of the aluminum angle fence. These holes will allow you to attach the replaceable zero-clearance fence with No. 8 × ⁵⁄₈" screws.

Fence Face

The fence face needs to grip the work securely. Otherwise your cuts have little hope of being square. You can choose

either of these following two options or use both together.

Cover the face of the fence with 120-grit adhesive-backed sandpaper. Or knock a couple of finishing nails into the back side of the fence until the tips point out about ¹⁄₃₂" or so. Clip off whatever remains on the other side and screw the fence to the aluminum angle.

Squaring and Modifications

This jig is simple to square. First, loosen the cap screws on your jig. Place the handle of an engineer's square against the edge of the sled's base that you trimmed earlier. Put the blade of the square against your fence and line things up. Tighten the cap screws. The nylon washers will allow you to snug them up really tight. Make a test-cut and check your results with the square.

For me, it was square after the first time — a huge improvement compared to the fussing necessary with our sliding table.

As built, this jig works great. One

modification you might want to consider down the road is adding a handle at the back. If your arms are short, a handle will help you push the jig through the last part of your crosscut while still keeping the work pressed against the jig's fence. The handle can be as simple as a ³⁄₄"-diameter dowel screwed to the tail end of the miter bar.

If you need to hang this sled on the wall, be sure to drill a hole or two in the sled's base. Finally, it's a good idea to clamp an extra piece of ³⁄₄" MDF on the other side of your blade. This will catch falloff pieces, preventing them from getting flung back at you.

This newest addition to our shop works surprisingly well. In fact, the only time I miss the sliding table system is when I need to miter big panels (an infrequent operation in our shop). Now, if only we could find some way to shrink the scrap pile in our shop, then we'd really have some room to move around.

Table Saw Powered by a Circular Saw

A ripping tool for the job site.

BY NICK ENGLER

I know — what idiot would use a homemade jig to saw when he's got a perfectly good Shopsmith sitting around? Well, the sort of idiot who writes articles about jigs and fixtures, I guess. But there's a good explanation; really, there is. First of all, that Shopsmith just got here. When Al Parrish took these photos in the new Wright Brothers Aeroplane Company workshop, Shopsmith had just delivered the tools. For a couple of months previous, while we were building the workshop, this circular saw table was the closest thing I had to a table saw — and it did just fine.

Like any craftsman with a well-equipped shop, I sometimes find myself at a disadvantage when I work at a job site and have to leave my stationary machines behind. And the tool I miss the most is a table saw, especially when I have a ripping operation to perform. So I made this jig to serve as my table saw away from my table saw.

Note that the saw table lays across one sawhorse, so the front and back of the table are parallel to the sawhorse. This keeps the table from sagging in the middle. The other sawhorse, which isn't shown in the photo, is perpendicular to the first and parallel to the sides of the table.

Making the Saw Table

It's an absurdly simple jig, as you can see. The saw table is a large piece of ¼" plywood, braced flat with a hardwood frame. The circular saw mounts to the table near one corner and is held in place by the frame and several cleats. The fence is a large T-square that clamps to the table. The table and T-square are large enough that I can rip to the center of a 48"-wide sheet of plywood.

When you make the table, you have to adjust the frame and the table cutout to fit your circular saw. As shown on the plan view, part of the frame forms a box around the table cutout. The interior dimensions of this box should be the same size as the outside dimensions of your circular saw base. The base should fit inside this box with little or no room to spare. Important note: Make sure that the frame members run true and are square to the edges of the saw table. When you install the saw, rest the edge of the base against the frame members.

The frame, cleats and the cutout all have to be adjusted to fit your particular circular saw. Notice that the side member of the frame is notched to accommodate the motor for this particular circular saw.

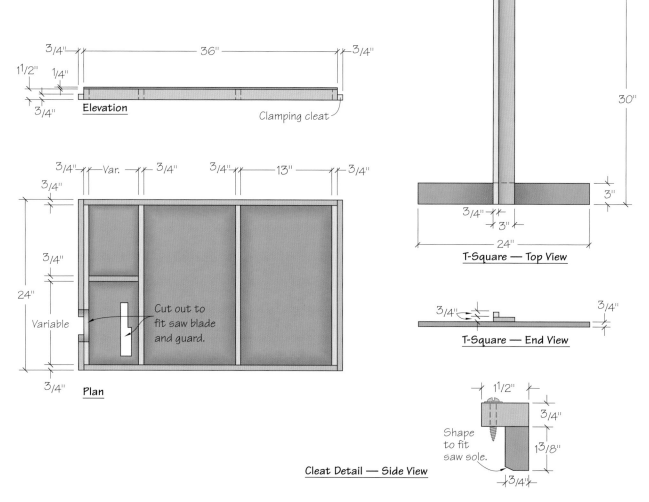

3/4" — 36" — 3/4"
1 1/2" 1/4"
3/4"
Elevation
Clamping cleat

3/4" — Var. — 3/4"   3/4" — 13" — 3/4"
3/4"
3/4"
24"
Variable
Cut out to fit saw blade and guard.
3/4"
Plan

30"
3"
3/4"
3"
24"
T-Square — Top View

3/4"   3/4"
T-Square — End View

1 1/2"
3/4"
13/8"
Shape to fit saw sole.
3/4"
Cleat Detail — Side View

If the assembly is square, the blade will be square to the front and back of the table. This, in turn, will make it easier to align the fence.

Secure the saw base in the jig with three or four L-shape cleats screwed to the frame members. Because the front edge of a circular saw base is often turned up to prevent it from catching as you push it over the wood, you might have to shape one edge of the cleat to fit the base. You might also have to cut a notch in a portion of the frame to accommodate the saw motor when the blade is extended for its maximum depth of cut.

Make the cutout using a jigsaw after you assemble the saw table and frame. The cutout must accommodate both the blade and the guard. You'll find that this saw table is just as handy upside down as it is right side up, and you don't want to accidentally set the saw table on the ground while the blade is still spinning. Not only will this dull the blade, it makes your toes very nervous.

Finally, make the T-square fence. Take care to align the bar square to the head.

Using the Saw Table: Upside Down or Right Side Up?

Each time you use the circular saw table, think through the operation before you begin cutting. Decide whether it would be easier and safer to use this jig as a table saw (feeding the wood into the blade) or as an extended base (pushing the saw and the jig across the wood; see the photo below). The smaller the workpiece, the more likely you are to use the jig as a table saw.

To do this, rest the jig on sawhorses. Put the horses together in a T shape, butting the end of one horse against the side of the other. Position the saw table so the long dimension lays across one sawhorse and the edge furthest from the saw rests on the other sawhorse. Clamp the long cleats at the sides of the table to the sawhorses.

Important safety consideration: When using the jig as a saw table, the saw switch will be under the table where you can't get to it quickly. To turn the saw on and off safely, either invest in a shielded foot switch or make a switch box and mount it to the side of the saw table where you can reach it easily in case of an emergency.

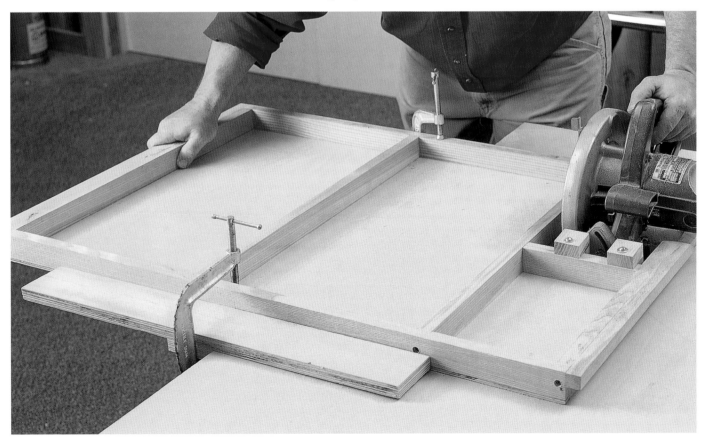

PROJECT

8

Table Saw Sled With Adjustable Stop

Making accurate cutoffs is business as usual for this slick fixture.

BY JIM STACK

The table saw is perfect for making accurate and repetitive crosscuts. This crosscut sled is the best tool for making those cuts safely and easily. It's large enough to make a 24" crosscut. The adjustable stop has a flipper, so only one setting is necessary to cut both ends of a board to length.

Cut the sled table to size and rout the two handle slots. Center the sled on the saw table, locate the left-milled slot in the saw top and mark its location on the sled. At the mark, draw a line square to the long edge of the sled table. Mount one runner along the line with flathead screws. Put the sled on the table saw and fine-tune the fit of the runner, using a scraper or chisel. When it slides smoothly in the slot, mark the location of the other slot. Mount the second runner and check the fit on the table saw. When the sled slides smoothly, apply wax to the underside.

Cut the front fence and rear stiffener pieces and shape per the drawing. Cut the slot in the front fence and mill a ¼" × ¼" rabbet on the bottom inside edge. Center the rear stiffener on the sled and attach it with 2" screws. Center the front fence and attach it at each end, using screws in slotted holes. Raise the saw blade, set the sled in place and carefully cut the kerf in the sled. Set a carpenter's square against the front fence

and adjust the fence until it is square to the saw kerf. Square the fence vertically to the sled table and attach with 2" screws. Cut and shape the safety block and attach it to the sled.

With the stop block cut to size, set it against the inside of the front fence and mark the hole for the carriage bolt so it lines up with the slot. Set the bolt in the

block, check the fit of the block to the fence and attach the knob. Attach the flipper so it can be pivoted up and freely dropped back into place.

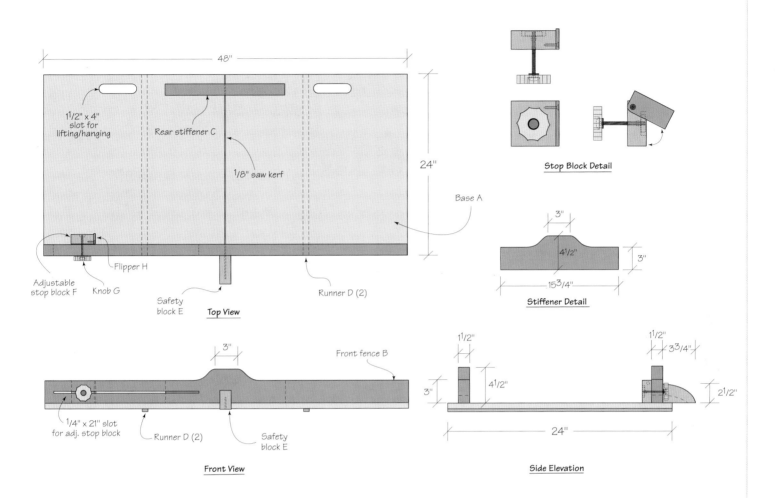

Top View

1 1/2" x 4" slot for lifting/hanging

Rear stiffener C

1/8" saw kerf

Base A

Adjustable stop block F

Knob G

Flipper H

Safety block E

Runner D (2)

Stop Block Detail

Stiffener Detail

3"

4 1/2"

15 3/4"

3"

48"

24"

Front View

1/4" x 21" slot for adj. stop block

Runner D (2)

Safety block E

Front fence B

3"

Side Elevation

1 1/2"

4 1/2"

3"

1 1/2"

3 3/4"

2 1/2"

24"

inches (millimeters)

REFERENCE	QUANTITY	PART	STOCK	THICKNESS	(mm)	WIDTH	(mm)	LENGTH	(mm)
A	1	base	plywood	3/4	(19)	24	(610)	48	(1219)
B	1	front fence	plywood	1 1/2	(38)	4 1/2	(114)	47 1/2	(1207)
C	1	rear stiffener	plywood	1 1/2	(38)	4 1/2	(114)	14	(356)
D	2	runners	hardwood	5/16	(8)	3/4	(19)	15 3/4	(400)
E	1	safety block	plywood	1 1/2	(38)	2 3/4	(70)	24	(610)
F	1	adjustable stop block	hardwood	1 1/4	(32)	3	(76)	3 3/4	(95)
G	1	knob	plywood	3/4	(19)	2 1/4 d	(57)		
H	1	flipper	hardwood	1/4	(6)	1 3/8	(35)	3	(76)

HARDWARE

17	No. 8 × 1 1/4" (No. 8 × 32mm) wood screws
1	3" × 1/4"–20 (76mm × 6mm–20) carriage bolt
1	1/4"–20 (6mm–20) T-nut
1	1/4" (6mm) fender washer
10	No. 8 × 2" (No. 8 × 51mm) wood screws

Tapering Fixture

You'll have the right slant on things using this fixture.

BY JIM STACK

Tapering fixtures come in many different sizes and shapes. This fixture incorporates a couple of features that make it safer.

Begin by cutting out all the parts as shown in the materials list. Join the two arms using a butt hinge, and attach the stop block to the adjustable arm. Then, attach the fixed arm to the bottom plate. Install the hanger bolt in the fixed arm, attach the slotted metal strap to the adjustable arm and hook it over the hanger bolt. Install the knob and attach the two toggle clamps to the adjustable arm.

This fixture is safe to use because the toggle clamps hold the part being cut securely to the bottom plate.

Lay the two arms flat on a bench and install the hinge. The space between the ends of the arms is equal to the diameter of the hinge barrel.

Install the hanger bolt in the fixed arm, put the slotted strap over it and put the pivot screw in place.

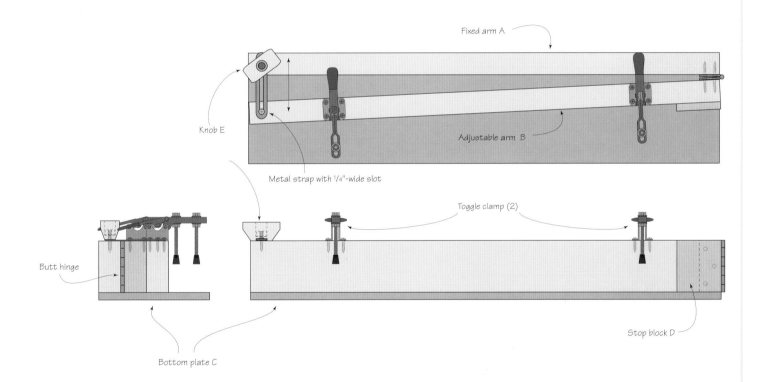

Fixed arm A

Knob E

Metal strap with 1/4"-wide slot

Adjustable arm B

Toggle clamp (2)

Butt hinge

Bottom plate C

Stop block D

inches (millimeters)

REFERENCE	QUANTITY	PART	STOCK	THICKNESS	(mm)	WIDTH	(mm)	LENGTH	(mm)
A	1	fixed arm	plywood	1	(25)	3 1/2	(89)	32	(813)
B	1	adjustable arm	plywood	1	(25)	3 1/2	(89)	32	(813)
C	1	bottom plate	plywood	1/2	(13)	7 1/2	(191)	32	(813)
D	1	stop block	hardwood	3 1/2	(89)	2 1/4	(57)	3	(76)
E	1	knob	hardwood	1 1/2	(38)	2	(51)	2 1/2	(64)

HARDWARE

1 3" × 3 1/2" (76mm × 89mm) butt hinge
2 toggle clamps
1 metal strap with 1/4"-wide (6mm-wide) slot
1 No. 8 × 3/4" (No. 8 × 19mm) wood screw
1 1 1/2" × 1/4"–20 (38mm × 6mm–20) hanger bolt

Tenoning Fixture

This is a "groovy" fixture because it will work on any table saw top with miter slots.

BY JIM STACK

Here's a tenoning fixture that will work on any table saw. First, cut all the parts as shown in the materials list. Then, cut a $\frac{1}{4}$" × 6" slot centered in the top plate. Attach the fence to the top plate and the fence alignment strip to the end of the top plate.

Attach the hardwood runner to the bottom of the base plate (see the illustration for details).

Set the fence assembly on the base plate and mark the location for the hanger bolt. Install the hanger bolt. Cut out the knob, drill it for the T-nut and install the T-nut. Then, put the fence assembly in place on the base plate, with the hanger bolt sticking up through the slot in the top plate. Be sure the fence assembly slides smoothly on the base plate. Make adjustments if necessary, then screw the knob in place.

Attach the right-angle braces from the bottom only. Put the fixture on the table saw and check the fence for square to the table of the saw (step 1).

Finally, attach the vertical guide (step 2).

1 Attach the right-angle braces to the top plate only. Then put the fixture on the table saw and check the fence for square to the saw table. Make adjustments as necessary and attach the braces to the fence.

2 Square the vertical guide to the saw table and attach it to the fence with screws.

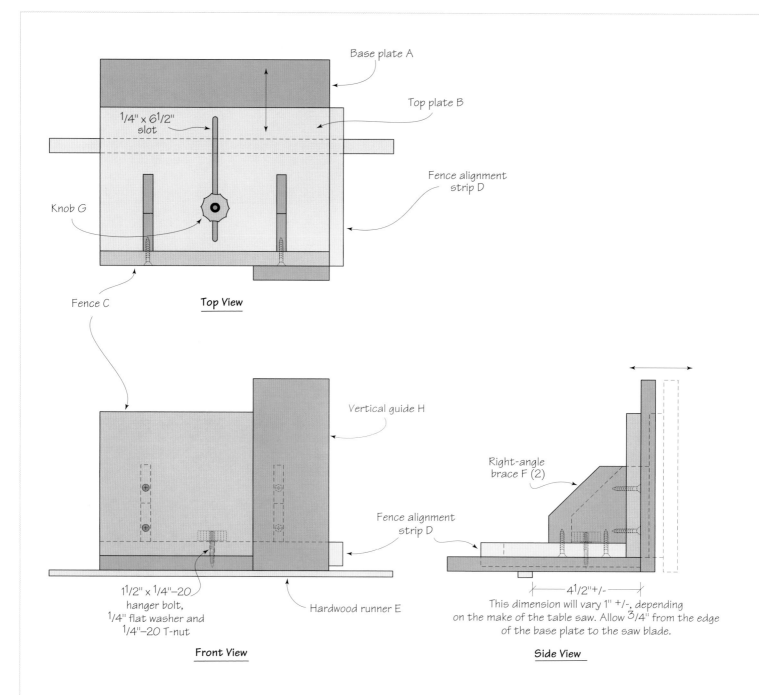

Base plate A

Top plate B

1/4" x 6 1/2" slot

Fence alignment strip D

Knob G

Fence C

Top View

Vertical guide H

Fence alignment strip D

1 1/2" x 1/4"–20 hanger bolt, 1/4" flat washer and 1/4"–20 T-nut

Hardwood runner E

Front View

Right-angle brace F (2)

4 1/2"+/-

This dimension will vary 1" +/-, depending on the make of the table saw. Allow 3/4" from the edge of the base plate to the saw blade.

Side View

inches (millimeters)

REFERENCE	QUANTITY	PART	STOCK	THICKNESS	(mm)	WIDTH	(mm)	LENGTH	(mm)
A	1	base plate	plywood	3/4	(19)	10	(254)	12	(305)
B	1	top plate	plywood	3/4	(19)	7 1/2	(191)	12	(305))
C	1	fence	plywood	3/4	(19)	7 1/2	(191)	12	(305)
D	1	fence alignment strip	plywood	3/4	(19)	1 1/4	(32)	8 1/4	(210)
E	1	hardwood runner	hardwood	3/8	(10)	3/4	(19)	18	(457)
F	2	right-angle braces	plywood	3/4	(19)	4	(102)	4	(102)
G	1	knob	plywood	3/4	(19)	2 1/4 dia	(57)		
H	1	vertical guide	plywood	3/4	(19)	4	(102)	10	(254)

HARDWARE

8   No. 8 × 1 1/4" (No. 8 × 32mm) wood screws

3   No. 6 × 3/4" (No. 6 × 19mm) wood screws

1   1 1/2" × 1/4"–20 (38mm × 6mm–20) hanger bolt

1   1/4"–20 (6mm–20) T-nut

1   1/4"(6mm) flat washer

PROJECT

11

Adjustable Router Base

This jig does more tricks than a dog and pony show.

BY JACK RICH

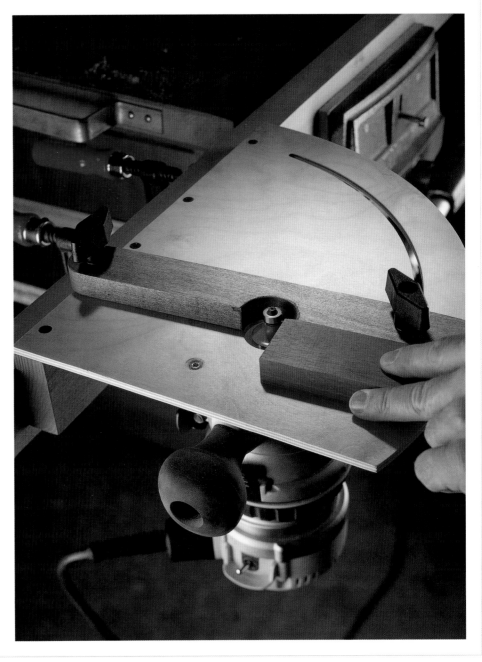

The jig is simply an auxiliary router base with an adjustable fence for edging or cutting rabbets and dadoes. I added a support piece to make it possible to clamp the unit to a 2×4 sawhorse beam. It can also be clamped in a woodworker's vise. This provides a small portable router table that can be easily taken to the job site.

The beauty of the fence is that it requires only one end to be moved to adjust the distance from the bit to the fence. The range of that dimension is from flush to 4½" (depending on the diameter of the bit). If needed, a second fence can be constructed. The second fence could be longer and permit the use of stop blocks. I tried to trim all excess material from the unit, hence the short fence and the shape of the base. The base can easily be adapted to any common router base, including plunge routers.

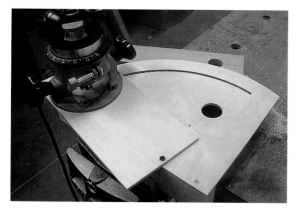

inches (millimeters)

REFERENCE	QUANTITY	PART	STOCK	THICKNESS	(mm)	WIDTH	(mm)	LENGTH	(mm)
A	1	base	plywood	1/4	(6)	10⁷/₈	(276)	14	(356)
B	1	fence	hardwood	3/4	(19)	1¹/₂	(38)	10⁷/₈	(276)
C	1	support	hardwood	3/4	(19)	2¹/₂	(64)	14	(356)

HARDWARE

3	No. 8 × 1¹/₂" (No. 8 × 38mm) flathead wood screws
1	1¹/₂" × ¹/₄"–20 (38mm × 6mm–20) carriage bolt
1	1¹/₂" × ¹/₄"–20 (38mm × 6mm–20) hanger bolt
2	¹/₄"–20 (6mm–20) wing nuts or threaded knobs
2	¹/₄"(6mm) flat washers

Cut the parts per the cutting list. Attach the hardwood support to the base. Drill a router-cutter clearance hole in a scrap piece of wood. Center the router base over this hole and attach it to the scrap. Install a ¹/₄" straight-cut router bit in the router and attach the router to its base. Measure 8⁷/₈" from the edge of the router bit to the opposite end of the scrap wood and drill a pivot-screw hole. Attach this router assembly to the adjustable jig base at the point where the hanger bolt will be inserted (see illustration). Cut the groove for the fence. Install the hanger bolt, attach the hardwood fence and you're ready to go.

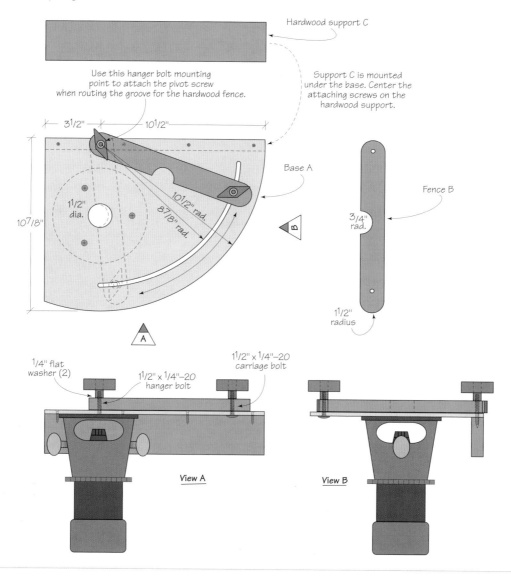

Hardwood support C

Use this hanger bolt mounting point to attach the pivot screw when routing the groove for the hardwood fence.

Support C is mounted under the base. Center the attaching screws on the hardwood support.

3¹/₂" 10¹/₂"

Base A

Fence B

1¹/₂" dia.

10¹/₂" rad.

8⁷/₈" rad.

3/4" rad.

10⁷/₈"

1¹/₂" radius

A

B

¹/₄" flat washer (2)

1¹/₂" × ¹/₄"–20 hanger bolt

1¹/₂" × ¹/₄"–20 carriage bolt

View A

View B

Face-Routing System

You'll put on a happy face when you see this jig system in action.

BY HARVEY FREEMAN

A painted cabinet door can be made from medium-density fiberboard (MDF) and given a raised-panel effect with a routed groove. This face-routing setup provides a system to guide the router and achieve a uniform margin on all four edges of the panel.

The system consists of four identical guides made from a base plate and an edge guide. The length of the guides should be as long as the longest part you plan to make.

Cut out all parts and be sure the edge guides have one good straight edge. Attach the guides to the base plates with nails or screws. Locate the guides at least 1" from the edge of the base plate.

When setting up the system, arrange the four guides like a pinwheel around the work. A flat work surface is the ideal place to set up this system. Be sure the guides on the base plates are close enough together so the router base plate will ride into and out of the corner smoothly.

You are limited only by your imagination as to how you can use this system. The door in the photo on the right, below, is made in two steps. First, the profile is routed in the front of the door. Then the rabbet is routed on the back of the door. As the rabbet is completed, the panel will drop out.

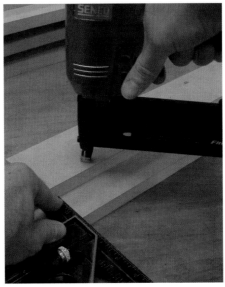

Attach the guides with nails or screws.

When the second cut is made, the center panel will drop out and can be easily removed from the door.

Different-size router bases can be easily made on a stationary sander (see the illustration). These bases can be used to position the router in different locations on the door faces with reference to the guide rails.

A flat worktop is ideal for using this system. The guide assemblies are screwed to the top.

This is a door that has been routed for a glass panel.

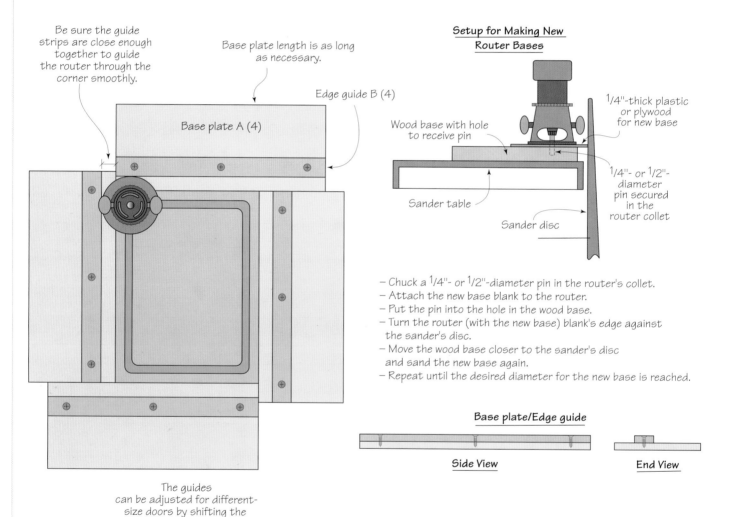

Be sure the guide strips are close enough together to guide the router through the corner smoothly.

Base plate length is as long as necessary.

Edge guide B (4)

Base plate A (4)

The guides can be adjusted for different-size doors by shifting the pinwheel setup.

Setup for Making New Router Bases

Wood base with hole to receive pin

1/4"-thick plastic or plywood for new base

1/4"- or 1/2"-diameter pin secured in the router collet

Sander table

Sander disc

– Chuck a 1/4"- or 1/2"-diameter pin in the router's collet.
– Attach the new base blank to the router.
– Put the pin into the hole in the wood base.
– Turn the router (with the new base) blank's edge against the sander's disc.
– Move the wood base closer to the sander's disc and sand the new base again.
– Repeat until the desired diameter for the new base is reached.

Base plate/Edge guide

Side View

End View

inches (millimeters)

REFERENCE	QUANTITY	PART	STOCK	THICKNESS	(mm)	WIDTH	(mm)	LENGTH	(mm)	COMMENTS
A	4	base plates	MDF	3/4	(19)	6	(152)	24	(610)	length is as long as necessary
B	4	edge guides	MDF	3/4	(19)	2	(51)	24	(610)	length is as long as necessary

HARDWARE

16   No. 8 × 1 1/4" (No. 8 × 32mm) flathead wood screws

Jig for Routing Circles

Cutting corners has never been so easy.

BY JIM STACK

This jig will hold your router securely and allow you to rout circles and arcs. The routing radius can be easily and precisely adjusted.

Start by cutting the parts as shown in the cutting list. Cut the ¼" slot in the arm plate, using a router mounted under a table.

Shape the base plate to the general shape shown in the illustration. Make sure the base plate is large enough for your router base. Glue the spacer plate to the base plate. Then, using screws, attach this assembly to the arm plate.

Drill a shallow counterbore in one of the ¼"-thick adjustable plates to accept the nail head. This will allow the nail head to seat flush to the surface of the plate. Drill a pilot hole for the nail shank. Cut the nail ¾" long and round the point. Insert the nail into the plate.

Drill a counterbore in another of the ¼"-thick adjustable plates to accept the head of the T-nut. Then drill the pilot hole for the barrel of the T-nut. Insert the T-nut into this plate. The head of the T-nut should be flush with the surface of the plate.

Glue all three of the ¼"-thick adjustable plates together. Sandwich the blank plate between the other two plates, as shown in the illustration. Be careful not to get any glue in the threads of the T-nut.

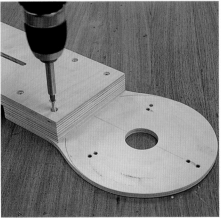

Drill a ¾"-diameter hole ¼" deep in the knob block. Shape the knob as shown, or to the shape you desire. Insert the carriage bolt in the knob. After you insert the threads of the carriage

bolt into the T-nut in the adjustable plate, tighten the knob. This will seat the square shoulder of the carriage bolt in the knob.

Remove the base plate on your

router and use it as a drilling template to drill the screw holes into the base plate of the fixture. Countersink for the base plate mounting screws and install the router base on the fixture base plate.

To use this fixture, determine the radius you want to rout. With the router attached to the jig, measure from the inside of the router bit to the center of the nail in the adjustable block and tighten the adjustable block. Drill a pivot hole in your workpiece, insert the nail in the hole and you're ready to rout.

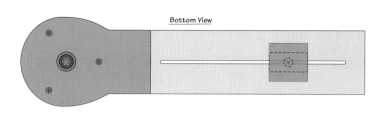
Bottom View

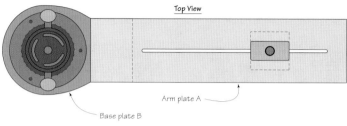
Top View

Arm plate A

Base plate B

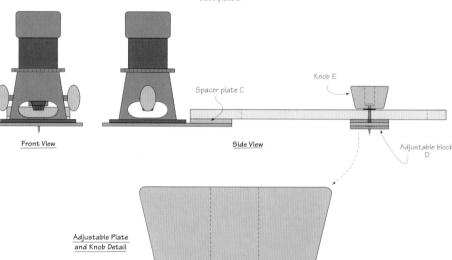

Front View Side View

Spacer plate C

Knob E

Adjustable block D

Adjustable Plate and Knob Detail

$1^{1}/_{2}$" × $^{1}/_{4}$"–20 carriage bolt

Three layers of $^{1}/_{4}$" × 3" × 3" plywood

$^{1}/_{4}$"–20 T-nut

Roofing nail cut to $^{3}/_{4}$" long

HARDWARE

1	$1^{1}/_{2}$" × $^{1}/_{4}$"–20 (38mm × 6mm–20) carriage bolt
1	$^{1}/_{4}$"–20 (6mm–20) T-nut
1	$^{1}/_{4}$" (6mm) fender washer
1	$1^{1}/_{4}$" (32mm) roofing nail (or any large-headed nail)
4	No. 8 × $1^{1}/_{4}$" (No. 8 × 32mm) wood screws

inches (millimeters)

REFERENCE	QUANTITY	PART	STOCK	THICKNESS	(mm)	WIDTH	(mm)	LENGTH	(mm)	COMMENTS
A	1	arm plate	plywood	$^{3}/_{4}$	(19)	5	(127)	20	(508)	
B	1	base plate	plywood	$^{1}/_{4}$	(6)	7	(178)	$10^{1}/_{2}$	(267)	
C	1	spacer plate	plywood	$^{1}/_{2}$	(13)	$3^{1}/_{2}$	(89)	5	(127)	
D	1	adjustable block	plywood	$^{3}/_{4}$	(19)	3	(76)	3	(76)	plate made from three $^{1}/_{4}$" × 3" × 3" (6mm × 76mm × 76mm) pieces of plywood (see drawing)
E	1	knob	plywood	$^{3}/_{4}$	(19)	2	(51)	2	(51)	shape knob after drilling hole for T-nut

Jig for Routing Ellipses

Using this jig is so much fun it's almost a crime.

BY JIM STACK

An ellipse is an angled cross section of a cone and has constantly changing radii. This jig will enable you to cut patterns, grooves and templates. A perfect ellipse will be the result every time.

This jig can easily be sized larger. Determine how large your ellipse will be and cut the base plate to size. The grooves for the guide blocks will be the same size regardless of the base plate dimensions.

To begin, cut the base plate to size. Then set up a dado cutter in your table saw and cut the grooves for the guide blocks. Center the grooves on the base plate.

Cut out the pivot arm. Use a router mounted under a router table to cut the 1/4" slot in the pivot arm. Next, cut out the guide blocks and drill them to accept the machine screws. (See the illustration for details.)

The mounting plate for the router that attaches to the pivot arm will vary in size and shape according to the size of your router.

Waxing the guide blocks and the guide block grooves will allow this jig to operate smoothly.

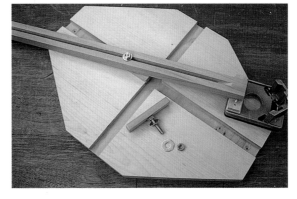

1 This photo shows the router base mounted to the pivot arm and one of the guide blocks, with all its parts. The mounting plate for the router will vary from router to router. The router base shown here is for a trim router.

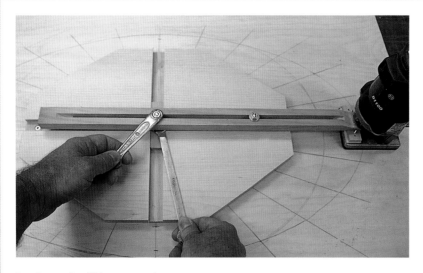

2 When setting up the jig, adjust the guide blocks to the length and width of the ellipse. Tighten the nuts so the blocks are locked in place on the pivot arm. Remember that the guide blocks need to be able to turn freely.

HARDWARE

2   2" × ¼"–20 (51mm × 6mm–20) oval head bolts
4   ¼"–20 (6mm–20) hex nuts
6   ¼" (6mm) flat washers

inches (millimeters)

REFERENCE	QUANTITY	PART	STOCK	THICKNESS	(mm)	WIDTH	(mm)	LENGTH	(mm)	COMMENTS
A	1	base plate	plywood	¾	(19)	11	(279)	16	(406)	
B	1	pivot arm	hardwood	¾	(19)	1¼	(32)	20	(508)	
C	2	guide blocks	hardwood	½	(13)	¾	(19)	3	(76)	
D	1	mounting plate	hardwood	½	(13)	¾	(19)	3	(76)	varies in size and shape according to the size of your router

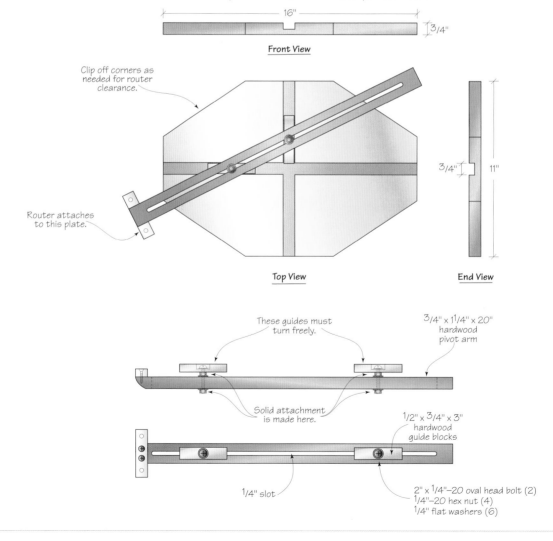

Dimensions of base plate can be adjusted to fit your particular needs.

16"
¾"
Front View

Clip off corners as needed for router clearance.

Router attaches to this plate.

¾"   11"
Top View   **End View**

These guides must turn freely.

¾" × 1¼" × 20" hardwood pivot arm

Solid attachment is made here.

½" × ¾" × 3" hardwood guide blocks

¼" slot

2" × ¼"–20 oval head bolt (2)
¼"–20 hex nut (4)
¼" flat washers (6)

Self-Centering Router Jig

Keep your center with this simple but dead accurate jig.

BY JIM STACK

This jig really does work! With a few scraps of plywood and some screws and washers, you can build this self-centering router jig in 30 minutes or less.

Cut the parts as shown in the cutting list. Lay out the router base on the $1/4$" plywood and cut it to your desired shape. Remove the plastic base from your router and use it as a template to mark the center hole and screw holes on the plywood base.

It's important to have the router-base mounting holes located so they will center the router on the plywood base. Drill the screw holes as accurately as you can. Be sure to countersink the holes so the router-base mounting screw heads from your router will sit below the surface of the base. Drill the center router-bit clearance hole and glue the router base blocks in place as shown in the illustration.

Mark for the clearance holes in the ends of the end bars and the plywood router base. Drill these holes large enough so the screws can be inserted in them with no force. The bars and the base will pivot on the screws through these holes.

Mark for the pilot holes in the two side rails. Drill these holes and attach the end bars, but don't fully tighten the screws.

Mount the router to the plywood base. Then attach the plywood router base to the side rails.

Lay out the desired shape of the plywood base, then cut it to shape using the band saw.

Be sure the holes that mount the base to the router hold the router in the center of the plywood base. This will ensure the proper centering of the router in the jig.

To use the jig, put it on the piece to be mortised and close the jig until both side rails are tight against the sides. Then, tighten the screws on the end bars and the plywood base. Slide the jig along the piece to cut the mortise.

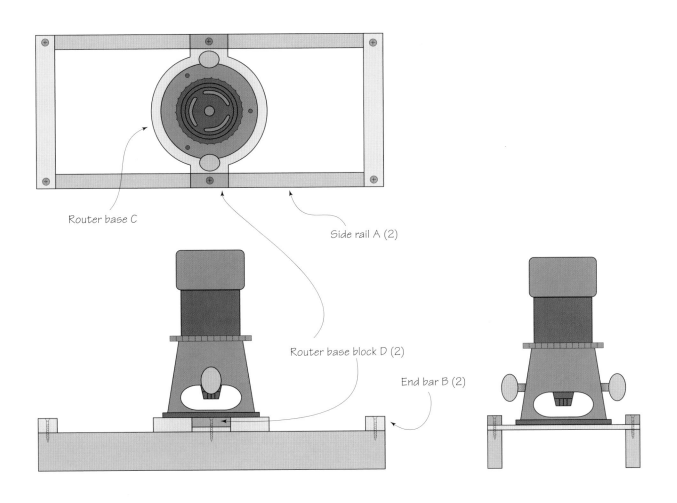

Router base C

Side rail A (2)

Router base block D (2)

End bar B (2)

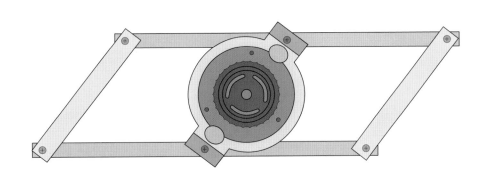

inches (millimeters)

REFERENCE	QUANTITY	PART	STOCK	THICKNESS	(mm)	WIDTH	(mm)	LENGTH	(mm)
A	2	side rails	plywood	$3/4$	(19)	2	(51)	12	(305)
B	2	end bars	plywood	$3/4$	(19)	1	(25)	8	(203)
C	1	router base	plywood	$1/4$	(6)	8	(203)	8	(203)
D	2	router base blocks	plywood	$1/2$	(13)	$3/4$	(19)	2	(51)

HARDWARE

6   No. 8 × $1^{1}/2$" (No. 8 × 38mm) roundhead wood screws

3   $3/16$" (5mm) flat washers

ROUTER

Shop-Made
Router Guides

For a few dollars' worth of acrylic and some hardware,
you can add a versatile and valuable system to your router
at a fraction of the cost of aftermarket guides.

BY MICHEL THERIAULT

The router is one of the most versatile tools in any shop. With the addition of this shop-made modular router base system, it will be even more valuable.

The router base system starts with a special offset base (a good thing by itself) that's designed to accept other accessories without having to remove your router from the base. It takes less than a minute to switch accessories, which include a circle jig, an edge guide and a flush-trimming attachment. An extension increases the maximum size of both the circle-cutting jig and the edge guide.

The Individual Pieces

The circle-cutting jig cuts circles from $2^{1}/_{2}$" to 20" in diameter simply by sliding the aluminum circle guide along the channel in the offset base. With the extension added, you can expand the circle-cutting capacity up to a full 56" diameter.

The edge guide works with any router that has the offset base attached. With it, you can adjust the edge guide from 0" to 7" from the center of the bit. Using the countersunk wood screw holes, you can add a larger wooden fence that's flush and below the edge of the guide. With the auxiliary wooden fence in place, the extension increases the maximum width of the edge guide to up to 20" from center.

The flush-trimming attachment added to the bottom of the offset base allows a straight bit to extend down (flush with the bottom of the attachment) to easily trim screw plugs, solid-wood edging and joints flush to the surface. The 90° angle on the base allows you to reach into tight corners.

Making the Templates

The key to making accurate parts is to make a template first out of $^{1}/_{2}$" medium-density fiberboard (MDF), then cut out the $^{3}/_{8}$"-thick acrylic pieces, using the MDF template to guide your router. Even if you make only one set of guides, this method will give you a high-quality shop-made jig.

We used $^{1}/_{2}$" MDF for the templates because it's stable and easy to work

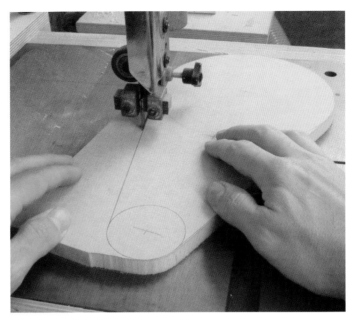

After transferring the template pattern to the template material, it takes only a minute to rough out the shape on the band saw. Cut as close to the line as you can to keep cleanup to a minimum.

For the interior holes in the template, hole-cutting saws, Forstner bits or spade bits will do the job. Make sure you back up the template to avoid blowout on the back side of the workpiece.

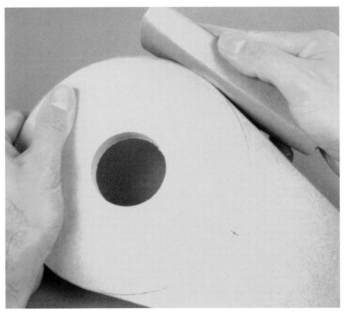

With everything cut, holed and sized appropriately, the last step is to clean up the edge so that it's smooth. A block and sandpaper can do most of the work, but an edge sander (if available) will be much quicker.

53

WORKING WITH ACRYLIC

Acrylic (also sold as Lexan or Plexiglas) is easy to cut with common woodworking machinery, such as table saws, scroll saws, band saws and routers. The single biggest problem is melting from an overheated cutter, so be aware of the feed rate and the heat generated when you are cutting acrylic. Also, the shavings will be heavily static charged and can make quite a mess, so don't use a dust collector when cutting acrylic.

When routing acrylic, you should use carbide-tipped bits because acrylic is abrasive. Keep the feed rates fast enough so the cut is smooth, without excessive buildup of heat. When routing the channels, such as those in the offset base and the extension, take light cuts and keep the feed rate fast, to reduce the possibility of melting.

Cut edges are sharp, so ease or break them with fine sandpaper, a file or even a roundover bit. You can also improve the look of cut edges by running a butane torch over the edge quickly to melt the edge slightly and remove the fine sandpaper and cutter marks.

Gluing acrylic requires a special glue (available from a plastics supply company) that literally melts the acrylic pieces together.

with. The $1/2$" allows enough thickness for the bearing on your router bit to ride against.

Each base piece has its own template. The offset base is made to comfortably fit most routers with 6"-diameter bases. If your router is larger, simply increase the diameter of the large end and lengthen the offset base by the amount necessary.

Offset Base Template

The offset base template requires a piece of MDF approximately 7" by 13" to allow for waste.

Using the diagrams as a guide, find the center by measuring in $3^1/2$" from one long edge at each end and make a mark. Join these marks to get the center line. Next, measure and make marks at 1", 6" and $9^1/4$" in from one end. Using a protractor, draw a 1"-radius circle from the 1" mark to define the small end. Then make a $3^1/4$"-radius circle from the $9^1/4$" mark to define the other end.

Using a ruler, connect the circles with two straight lines that touch the edges of both circles. This forms the basic shape of the base. Next, drill a $1/8$" hole at the 1" and 6" marks you previously drew.

Using a jigsaw or band saw, cut out the template, keeping just outside the line. Once the template is cut out, you can smooth the cut edges with a sanding block.

To finish the offset base template, use a 2"-diameter hole saw to drill the 2"

hole at the $9^1/4$" mark, centered in the large end of the offset base. Save the plug that comes out of the hole; it will be useful for centering the offset base when mounting it to your router. If you don't have a hole saw, you can cut the hole out with either a jigsaw or a scroll saw.

Flush-Trimming Attachment Template

Use the offset base template to make the template for the flush-trimming attachment. Start with a piece of MDF approximately 6" by 10". Attach this template blank to the offset base template with double-sided tape so that it overhangs the small end, and trim the blank to within $1/4$" of the template on your band saw. Use a $1/2$" template router bit with a top-mounted bearing in your table-mounted router to shape the outside edges of the template.

Next, drill $1/4$" holes through the flush-trimming template at the 1" and 6" locations, using the holes in the off-

set base template as a guide. Find the center of the 2" hole and mark that location. Follow the diagrams to draw two lines at right angles to each other, meeting at the center of the 2" hole. At the intersection, drill a hole slightly larger than the size of bit you will be using for flush cutting. Finally, cut along the two lines with a band saw or jigsaw and smooth with a sanding block.

Edge Guide Template

To make the edge guide template, first cut a rectangular piece of MDF 6" wide by 8" long. This is longer than needed so you can drill the 1"-radius cutout. To make the cutout, measure 3" in from the long edge and 5" from the end and make a mark. Cut a 2"-diameter hole with a hole saw, or other appropriate saw, at the mark. To finish the template, use your table saw or chop saw to cut the scrap from the end through the center of the 2" hole you just cut.

Measure and mark for the three holes as shown in the diagrams and drill all three holes with a $1/4$" drill bit, then sand all the edges smooth with a sanding block.

Extension Template

For the extension template, start with a piece of MDF exactly $2^1/2$" by 21" long. Choose one of the ends as a reference and make a mark in the exact center at 1", $4^1/2$", $6^1/4$" and $19^3/4$" from the reference end. Using a protractor, draw a $2^1/2$"-diameter circle at the $19^3/4$" mark shown on the drawing.

Cut out the round end of the template using a jigsaw or band saw. Drill a $1/4$" hole at each of the other marks as shown.

HARDWARE

1	$1/4$" (6mm) nylon washers, package of 10	item #00M40.23	Lee Valley
1	$2^1/4$" (57mm) pentagon knob	item #00M50.01	Lee Valley
3	$1^1/8$" (28mm) wing knobs	item #00M51.01	Lee Valley
1	1" (25mm) clamping knob	item #00M56.21	Lee Valley
3	1" × $1/4$"–20 (25mm × 6mm–20) hex-head bolts		
1	$1^1/4$" × $1/4$"–20 (32mm × 6mm–20) hex-head bolt		
2	1" × $1/4$"–20 (25mm × 6mm–20) flathead bolts		
1	$1/8$" × $3/8$" (3mm × 10mm) rolled steel pin		

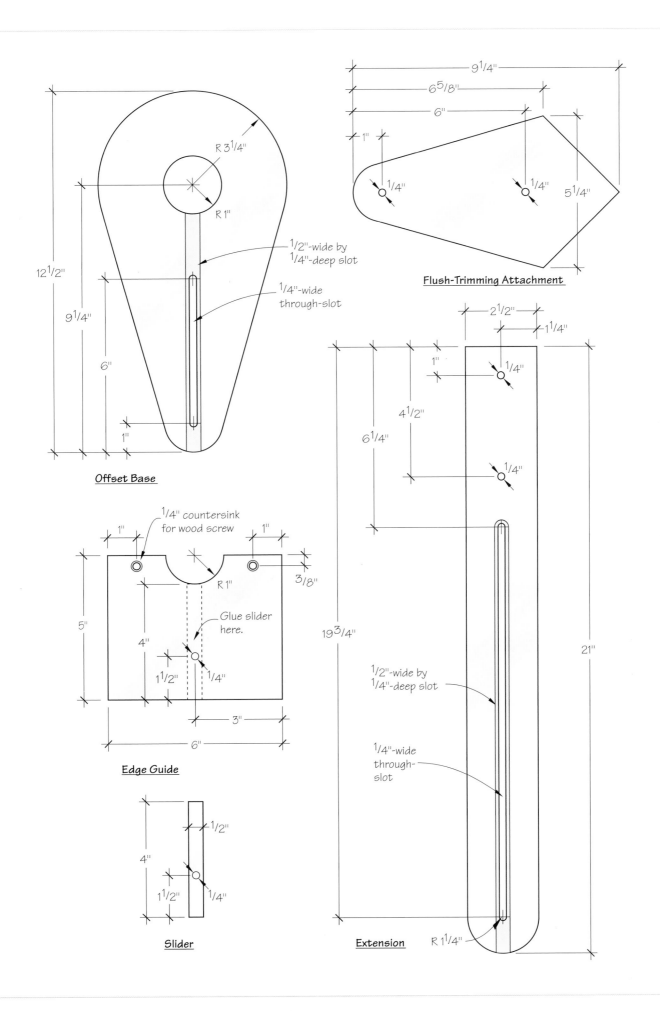

R 3¹/₄"

R 1"

¹/₂"-wide by ¹/₄"-deep slot

¹/₄"-wide through-slot

12¹/₂"

9¹/₄"

6"

1"

Offset Base

9¹/₄"

6⁵/₈"

6"

1"

¹/₄"

¹/₄"

5¹/₄"

Flush-Trimming Attachment

¹/₄" countersink for wood screw

1"

1"

R 1"

3/8"

Glue slider here.

5"

4"

1¹/₂"

¹/₄"

3"

6"

Edge Guide

¹/₂"

4"

¹/₄"

1¹/₂"

Slider

2¹/₂"

1¹/₄"

1"

¹/₄"

4¹/₂"

6¹/₄"

¹/₄"

19³/₄"

21"

¹/₂"-wide by ¹/₄"-deep slot

¹/₄"-wide through-slot

R 1¹/₄"

Extension

Making the Offset Base

All the bases are made from $3/8$"-thick (except for the slider piece, which is $3/16$" thick) acrylic, also sold as Lexan or Plexiglas. This can be commonly found at a local plastics store. Check the phone book in your area.

Before cutting the outer shape of the offset base, rout the slots into the acrylic while it is still rectangular. Start by measuring 1", 6" and $9\frac{1}{4}$" from one end and make marks at the center of the piece. These are reference marks for routing the slots. The first slot is $1/2$" wide and $1/4$" deep and goes from one edge to the $9\frac{1}{4}$" mark.

If you aren't able to find $3/16$" acrylic for the slider piece, $1/4$" can be used, but you'll either need to make this $1/4$"-deep groove slightly deeper, or recess the slider strip into a corresponding groove in the edge guide.

Using a $1/2$" router bit in your table-mounted router, set the fence $3\frac{1}{4}$" from the center of the bit. Run the groove in two $1/8$" passes, feeding the blank into the bit until it reaches the $9\frac{1}{4}$" mark.

Without moving the fence, replace the $1/2$" bit with a $1/4$" spiral carbide bit and set it $1/2$" high. If you have to remove the fence to change the bit, mark its exact position and set the fence back to the mark after changing the bit. It's important that the $1/4$" slot is centered in the $1/2$" slot.

Turn on the router and position the blank over the bit at the 1" mark. Slowly lower the blank onto the bit until it cuts all the way through, then carefully feed the blank into the bit until you reach the 6" mark.

With the slots cut, apply double-sided tape to one side of the template and, using $1/4$" bolts through the

holes in the template, position the template onto the acrylic blank so that the two $1/4$" holes in the template line up with the $1/4$" slot in the acrylic. Trim the acrylic on the band saw, then use the template bit to trim the base to the template.

Next, drill a $5/8$" or larger hole through the acrylic inside the 2" hole in the template in order to rout the 2" hole with the template bit already set in your table.

Finally, round over the bottom edges of the offset base with a $1/8$" roundover bit and sand the sharp edges with fine sandpaper.

Making the Flush-Trimming Attachment

Use the same steps as used on the offset base to trim the flush-trimming template to the acrylic blank. Using the $1/4$"

With the template carefully attached to the acrylic, use your band saw to rough out the shape of the jig itself. Leave a little extra, but don't leave so much that the router won't be able to clean it up easily.

After cutting an adequately sized starter hole with a drill bit, a bearing-guided flush-cutting bit does a nice job of shaping the interior holes to match the template.

Using the same bearing-guided flush-cutting bit, neatly trim the outside of the jig to the template.

I used a bearing-guided roundover bit to soften the bottom edges of the jigs to protect the wood from scratches and to protect the slightly fragile edges on the jig itself. For the rest of the edges, sandpaper works fine.

holes in the template as a guide, drill $\frac{1}{4}$" holes through the flush-trimming base. Knock off the sharp edges with fine sandpaper, then countersink the $\frac{1}{4}$" holes on one side to accommodate the flathead bolts.

Making the Extension

Similar to making the offset base, you need to rout the slots into the blank before you use the template. Choose a reference end and measure $6\frac{1}{4}$" and $19\frac{3}{4}$" from the end, scribing at each point a small mark centered on the blank to use as reference marks when you rout the slots. The first slot is $\frac{1}{2}$" wide and $\frac{1}{4}$" deep and goes from the end opposite the reference end to the $6\frac{1}{4}$" mark. Then follow the offset base steps to cut the slots.

With the slots cut, mount the template to the base and trim the acrylic, using first the band saw, then the template bit, breaking the edges with sandpaper afterwards.

Making the Edge Guide

Attach the edge guide template to the acrylic blank and follow the same procedures as before to trim the blank, using the band saw and a template bit in your router. Using the $\frac{1}{4}$" holes in the template as a guide, drill $\frac{1}{4}$" holes through the edge guide. Remove the template and break the sharp edges with fine sandpaper. Then countersink the two $\frac{1}{4}$" holes on the top of the guide to

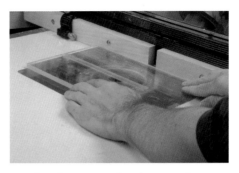

Running the grooves for the mounting hardware in both the offset base and the extension is a two-step operation. The $\frac{1}{4}$"-deep stopped groove is run first, using the router table fence to locate the slot in the center.

The through-slot is cut afterwards, again using the fence as a guide. You may be able to switch bits in the router without moving the fence and keep everything perfectly centered. If not, double-check the through-slot's location.

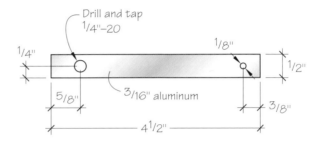

Drill and tap $\frac{1}{4}$"–20 · $\frac{1}{4}$" · $\frac{1}{8}$" · $\frac{1}{2}$" · $\frac{5}{8}$" · $\frac{3}{16}$" aluminum · $\frac{3}{8}$" · $4\frac{1}{2}$"

accommodate wood screws.

Cut a strip of $\frac{3}{16}$" acrylic slightly under $\frac{1}{2}$" wide on your table saw and then cut it 4" long. Place the strip in the slot on the extension or offset base and drill the $\frac{1}{4}$" hole, using the $\frac{1}{4}$" slot as a guide to ensure it is centered. Using a square, carefully glue the strip to the top of the edge guide with acrylic glue. Make sure that the two holes line up by inserting a $\frac{1}{4}$"–20 bolt in the two holes.

Making the Circle Guide

The circle guide is made from $\frac{3}{16}$"-thick by $\frac{1}{2}$"-wide aluminum, brass, wood or acrylic. First, cut the bar to length. Test the fit in the slot on your offset base. It should slide easily, but not have too much play in it. File the width to fit, and test again.

Next, measure and mark for the two holes as shown. The hole $\frac{5}{8}$" from one end will be tapped to accommodate a $\frac{1}{4}$"–20 bolt. Drill the hole with a $1\frac{5}{32}$" drill bit, then use the $\frac{1}{4}$"–20 tap to make the threads. Drill the other hole with a $\frac{1}{8}$" drill.

Carefully position a rolled steel pin over the $\frac{1}{8}$" hole and hammer it into position until the top side is flush with the bar. When using the circle guide, slip a small brad nail through the rolled steel pin, tapping it into the center point of the wood being cut. Or you can drill a $\frac{1}{8}$" hole and use the rolled pin itself for your pivot point. Instant router compass!

ATTACHING YOUR ROUTER

It isn't critical that the offset base be positioned exactly center over the router bit; however, it should be as close as possible.

Because the hole pattern of each router is different, you will have to use your existing router plate to locate the holes for drilling. The simplest way is to remove your existing router plate and position it on top of the offset base. Keep track of the hole pattern in the router base relative to the handles and make sure they are lined up so that one handle is facing away from the long end of the offset base, but ensure that the other handle will not get in the way of the circle jig's knob.

Center the offset base by eye and scribe the locations of the holes. If you saved the plug from the hole saw, you can wrap masking tape around the plug until it fits snugly into the hole in the offset base and use the center hole for better accuracy when lining up the base plate holes.

Next, drill the holes the required diameter and countersink them as necessary. Depending on the thickness of your original base plate and the length of the original bolts, you may need to purchase longer bolts in order to attach the new offset base to your router.

ROUTER

Supersimple Dado-and-Rabbet Jig

Two pieces of wood and some hardware will speed you through making bookshelves, tenons and even breadboard ends.

BY NICK ENGLER

When building a bookcase, you often must make a series of repetitive dadoes in the long uprights to support the shelves. You could do this on a table saw with a dado blade, but you'll find it's difficult to control the long stock as you feed it over the blade. If you have a router, you could clamp a straightedge to the stock and use it to guide the router, but it's time-consuming to measure and set up for each individual cut.

The dado-and-rabbet jig simplifies both the setup and the operation. Lock the board between the base and clamping bar, then guide the router along the bar. The stock doesn't move, so you don't have to worry about controlling a large piece of wood. The straightedge is also the clamp, so the setup is simple.

And that's not all it does. The jig helps create any long dado, rabbet or slot. You can make repetitive cuts in multiple parts. And you can use it to guide other handheld tools, such as a jigsaw or a circular saw, to make straight cuts.

Cutting dadoes in long pieces of material is fast and easy with this simple jig.

To make a positioning gauge, clamp a piece of scrap under the clamping bar so you won't cut into the base. Rest a scrap of ¼" plywood or hardboard against the bar and secure it to the scrap with a separate clamp. Then rout through the material, saving the strip between the router bit and the clamping bar.

Use the positioning gauge to align the stock underneath the clamping bar. The edge of the gauge indicates the inside edge of the cut.

Making the Dado-and-Rabbet Jig

The jig is just two pieces of wood — a base and a clamping bar. The sizes of both parts are determined by your own needs. My jig is about as long as my workbench is wide. This allows me to clamp the ends of the base to the bench. Not only does this keep the jig from moving around while I'm using it, but it also keeps the base flat when I tighten the clamping bar against the stock to be routed.

Make the base from ¾" plywood and the clamping bar from a hard, dense wood such as oak or maple. The bar should be fairly thick from top to bottom so it doesn't bow when tightened down. If it bows, the clamping pressure won't be even all across the stock. In fact, the bar will press against the stock only at the edges and the stock will be more likely to slip. This becomes more and more of a problem the longer you make the clamping bar. To solve it, I crowned the top and bottom surfaces of the clamping bar, making it ¹⁄₃₂" to ¹⁄₁₆" thicker in the center than at the ends. Even though the bar flexes, the clamp-

ing pressure remains even. However, remember that the sides of the clamping bar (the surfaces that will guide your router) must be perfectly straight.

Tip: To keep the stock from shifting in the jig, apply self-adhesive sandpaper to the underside of the clamping bar. In some cases, you may also want to apply a strip of sandpaper to the base, directly under the bar.

Drill counterbored holes for the carriage bolts in both the base and the clamping bar. The counterbores in the base recess the heads of the bolts so the base will rest flat on the work-

bench. The counterbores in the clamping bar provide recesses for the compressed spring, allowing you to clamp thin stock.

The purpose of these springs, of course, is to automatically raise the bar every time you need to move or remove the stock. What do you do if you're routing thick stock and the springs don't reach far enough into the counterbores to raise the clamping bar? Simply turn the bar over so the springs are no longer recessed in the counterbores. (This, by the way, is why I crowned both the top and bottom of the bar.)

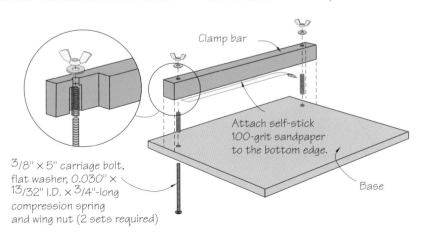

Clamp bar

Attach self-stick 100-grit sandpaper to the bottom edge.

Base

3/8" × 5" carriage bolt, flat washer, 0.030" × 13/32" I.D. × 3/4"-long compression spring and wing nut (2 sets required)

Making Dadoes and Rabbets

To use the jig, first you must position the stock on the base under the clamping bar. To do this quickly and accurately, it helps to make a positioning gauge from a scrap of thin plywood or hardboard. Lock the bar down on the base and place the scrap so one straight edge rests against the side of the bar. (The scrap must not be under the clamping bar.) Mount in your router the bit you will use to make the cuts, then rout all the way through the scrap, creating a strip about as long as the bar. The width of this strip is precisely the distance from the edge of the router to the cutting edge of the bit, and it becomes the positioning gauge for that specific router and that bit.

Lay out the cut you want to make, slide the stock beneath the bar, and turn the wing nuts so the bar is snug against the stock, but not tight. Place the positioning gauge against the clamping bar and line up your layout marks with the edge of the gauge. Then tighten the bar down and remove the gauge.

Rout the dado or the rabbet, keeping the router against the side of the clamping bar. This is like any other router operation (feed the router left to right as you face the bar so the rotation of the bit helps hold the router against the guiding edge). Make deep cuts in several passes, routing about 1/8" deeper with each pass.

If your router has a flat side to its base, keep that pressed against the fence. If the base is round, you may want to mount the router to a square sole for this operation. Router bits aren't always perfectly concentric to the sole, and the bit may move in and out slightly from the clamping bar if the router turns as you make the cut. This will make the cut curved or wavy.

The jig is not only useful for cutting dadoes and rabbets in wide stock, it's a time-saver for making identical cuts in multiple parts. You can line up the parts under that clamping bar and cut several at once. For example, you can make tenons in the ends of multiple door rails by cutting four identical rabbets in the end of each piece. To do this, first position two parts under the clamping bar, one near each end. Then clamp a short fence, no taller than the stock is thick, against the ends of the parts. This will automatically position the rails for each cut you make.

Line up several rails edge-to-edge with the ends against the fence and lock the bar down on top of them. Check to see that each part is secure. If it shifts, you may have to add another clamp behind the clamping bar. Rout the faces of the rails, then turn them over and repeat. After routing the faces, make identical cuts in the edges. If the router seems unstable when routing the edges, either wait until you have enough parts to stack face-to-face to make a larger platform for the router or put spacers between the parts to spread them out.

You can rout multiple parts by stacking them edge-to-edge or face-to-face. However, you must be careful that all the parts are secure under the clamping bar. If there is a slight discrepancy in the thickness of the pieces, one or more parts may shift during the cut. To prevent this, you may have to use additional clamps to secure individual pieces to the base.

To make multiple identical cuts, such as cutting the cheeks and shoulders of tenons in several rails, clamp a short fence to the base to automatically position the parts. Always check with the positioning gauge, however, before you make each cut.

PROJECT

18

Router Plane and Beader

Making these two terrific tools is simple using shop scraps and scrap metal.

BY NICK ENGLER

f you are asking yourself, "Making a what?" don't feel bad. I spent the first half of my woodworking career not even knowing what a router plane or a beader was — and the second half wondering how I did without them.

Simply put, a router plane cuts a groove, while a beader shapes an edge.

Together, these two simple hand tools do some of the same jobs that a hand-held electric router does. And they do them just as accurately with a minimum of setup time. In some applications, they are more capable and versatile than a router. And best of all, they won't cost diddly. You can make them in a few hours from scraps.

A beader (above left) is a great tool for hand-detailing furniture and is easier and safer than an electric router in some cases. A hand router plane (above right) excels at cutting hinge mortises and cleaning out grooves.

61

The trick to using the beader is to draw it along the wood in the opposite direction to which the blade is sloped, just like a scraper. Don't press too hard; light cuts will get you the results you want faster than heavy ones.

The Beader

A beader is a small scraper plane. But instead of scraping a flat surface, it scrapes a profile. Because it scrapes away such a small amount of stock with each pass, you don't have to worry about chipping or tear-out. Nor do you need to sand the shapes afterwards to remove mill marks. You can scrape smooth profiles in highly figured wood, if need be. You also can cut much smaller profiles and a greater variety of them than you can with a router. You can make a scraper blade from a worn-out hacksaw blade and file whatever shape you wish to make.

Create the body of the beader from a scrap of hardwood. Bevel the front edge at 10°, then cut dadoes in the front and bottom faces. Rough out the shape of the body by making a compound cut on a band saw. To do this, first trace both the top and front patterns of the body on the wood. Cut the top pattern first, then tape the waste back to the body. Cut the front pattern, discard the waste and round over the edges of the handles with a rasp so they fit your hands comfortably.

Also make a blade clamp and a fence. These simply screw onto the body. Note that the 1/4" fence can be mounted on either side of the blade, depending on the operation.

Beader

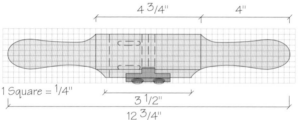

1 Square = 1/4"

4 3/4"   4"

3 1/2"

12 3/4"

Top View

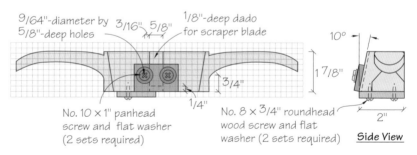

9/64"-diameter by 5/8"-deep holes

3/16" 5/8"

1/8"-deep dado for scraper blade

3/4"

1/4"

No. 10 × 1" panhead screw and flat washer (2 sets required)

No. 8 × 3/4" roundhead wood screw and flat washer (2 sets required)

10°

1 7/8"

2"

Side View

Front View

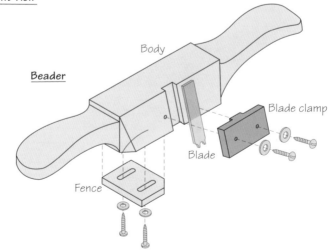

Beader

Body

Blade clamp

Blade

Fence

To use a beader, first make sure the blade is sharp. Lightly file the profile to create a burr or turn the burr with a burnisher, just as you would sharpen a scraper. When mounting the blade, set the depth and be sure the burr faces in, toward the body. Align the beader on the work with the beveled front facing away from you. Draw the tool toward you, applying light pressure, and the blade will remove a small amount of stock. Repeat until you have cut the profile to the desired depth.

The Router Plane

Like the beader, the iron of a router plane reaches down below the bottom of the tool. But this plane iron cuts rather than scrapes. If you're up for a little blacksmithing, you can make your own iron from a length of tool steel. (I made the iron shown here from drill stock.) You can also buy the irons from most mail-order woodworking catalogs.

While you can make the base from hardwood, I recommend clear plastic. This lets you see the cut as you make it. Cut the handle from very hard wood, such as rock maple. (I used a scrap of rosewood.) You need the hardness to cut threads for the thumbscrew. I've found that an ordinary metal tap works reasonably well when cutting small threads in hardwood, provided you don't need to tighten the threaded fastener much. I imagine the threads will eventually become too loose to hold the thumbscrew — mine is still tight after several years — but you can make a new handle simply enough.

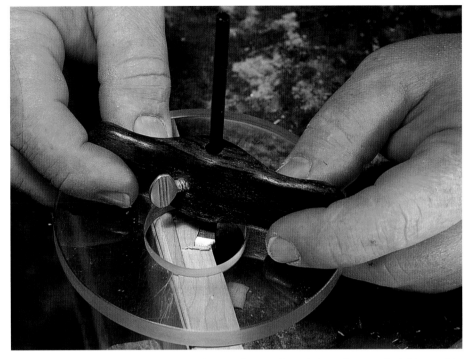

I've found that the plane seems to cut better if you "pivot" it into the wood. Hold one side of the handle stationary and push the other so the cutting edge swings in a small arc.

Mount the iron in the handle and set it to the desired depth of cut. Don't try to remove more than $1/32$" of stock at a pass; you get better results if you just shave the wood. I use my router plane for trimming the bottoms of dadoes, grooves and mortises when I need them just a little deeper. Where this tool shines is in making hinge mortises. In fact, you can use the edge of the hinge leaf as a gauge to set the depth of cut. Cut the outline of the mortise with a chisel, then shave away the waste with the router plane. The mortise will be perfectly flat across the bottom and just the right depth.

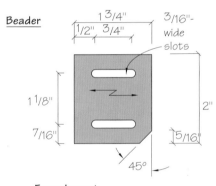

Beader

Fence Layout

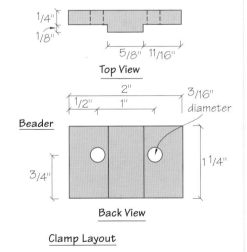

Top View

Beader

Back View

Clamp Layout

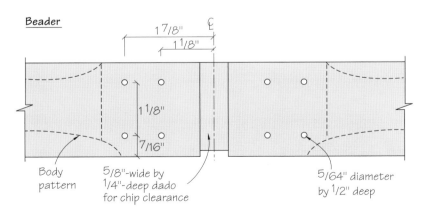

Beader

Body pattern

5/8"-wide by 1/4"-deep dado for chip clearance

5/64" diameter by 1/2" deep

Bottom Detail

<u>Router Plane</u>

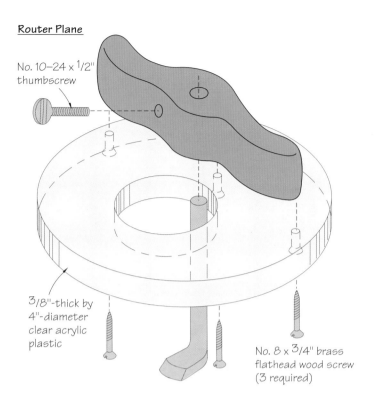

No. 10–24 x 1/2"
thumbscrew

3/8"-thick by
4"-diameter
clear acrylic
plastic

No. 8 x 3/4" brass
flathead wood screw
(3 required)

<u>Router Plane</u>

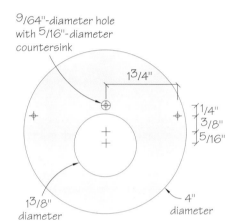

9/64"-diameter hole
with 5/16"-diameter
countersink

1 3/4"

1/4"
3/8"
5/16"

1 3/8"
diameter

4"
diameter

<u>Router Plane</u>

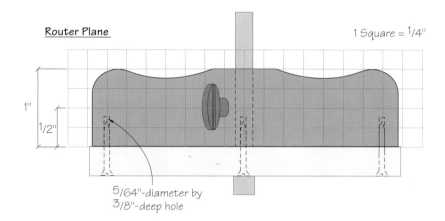

1 Square = 1/4"

1"

1/2"

5/64"-diameter by
3/8"-deep hole

<u>Front View</u>

<u>Router Plane</u>

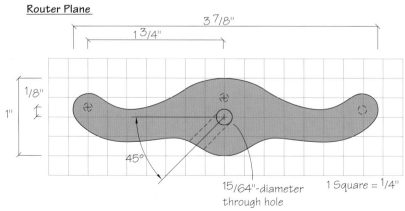

3 7/8"

1 3/4"

1/8"

1"

45°

15/64"-diameter
through hole

1 Square = 1/4"

<u>Top View</u>

Chisel-Sharpening Jig

With just a few scrap materials you can have a sharper approach to your work.

BY CHARLES STREET

This jig takes advantage of the fact that most good lathe knives or carving chisels have a metal ferrule at the business end of the handle. Drilling a hole of this exact diameter in the center of the jig's hub is a simple, yet effective way to anchor the tool at the grinder. The user now has three-way pivotal control over the tool and can restore the factory edge with confidence.

Since ferrule diameters often differ from one type of tool to another, interchangeable hubs are needed to accommodate different tools such as carving chisels. If it happens that the tool's blade is larger than the ferrule, such as a 1" skew, extra hub materials can be cut away to allow the tool to be inserted through the hub, and the jig will work fine provided there is sufficient circular bearing left to engage the ferrule.

Cut a piece of polyvinyl chloride (PVC) pipe for the collar, as indicated in the materials list. Drill a hole for the toilet bolt in the collar. Insert the bolt and tighten it. Then drill the holes for the dowels. Turn the hubs (step 1) and drill them for the dowels (step 2). Finally, drill the hub to accept the ferrule of the tool you want to sharpen.

Mount the jig on a scrap of wood and attach it to your grinder.

1 When turning the hub to fit inside the collar, turn several at the same time.

2 Center the dowel holes and use a clamp to hold the hub firmly at the drill press.

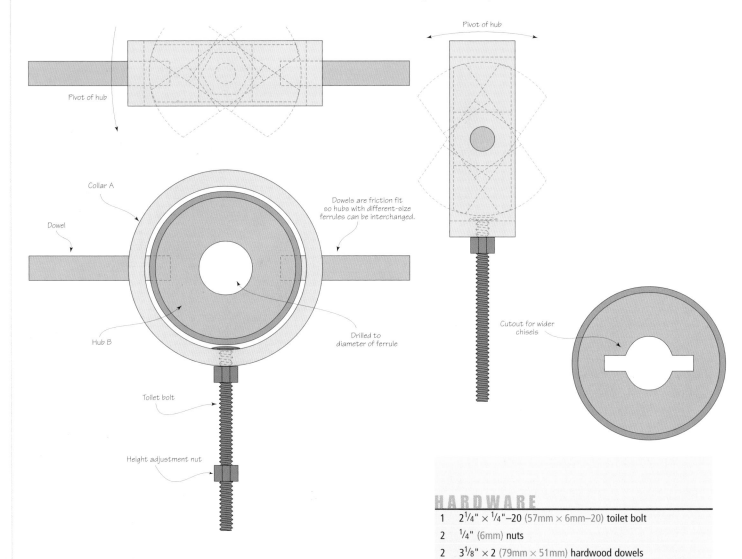

Pivot of hub

Pivot of hub

Pivot of hub

Collar A

Dowel

Dowels are friction fit so hubs with different-size ferrules can be interchanged.

Hub B

Drilled to diameter of ferrule

Toilet bolt

Height adjustment nut

Cutout for wider chisels

HARDWARE

1   2¼" × ¼"–20 (57mm × 6mm–20) toilet bolt

2   ¼" (6mm) nuts

2   3⅛" × 2 (79mm × 51mm) hardwood dowels

inches (millimeters)

REFERENCE	QUANTITY	PART	STOCK	THICKNESS	(mm)	WIDTH	(mm)	LENGTH	(mm)	COMMENTS
A	1	collar	PVC pipe			2 dia.	(51)	1	(25)	
B	1	turning blank	hardwood	2½	(64)	2½	(64)	6	(152)	turn several ⅞"-thick (22mm-thick) hubs to fit inside the collar

Dovetail Jig

Save yourself years of practice with this incredible jig that helps you hand-cut

BY JIM STUARD

Years ago when I first learned to cut dovetails, my first joints weren't things of beauty. Sometimes there were more shims than pins. Over time, my work got better and faster. But despite the improvement in my skills, I still had trouble cutting tails or pins consistently, especially if I got out of practice.

This jig allows you to make great dovetails on your first day. The idea came to me when I was building a Shaker step stool using hand-cut dovetails. I made a jig that fit over the end of a board to guide my saw through the cut and provide a perfect tail. The jig didn't cut pins and worked only on ³/₄"-thick boards. I guess I wasn't thinking big that day.

A few weeks later it came to me: Why not build a jig that cuts both tails and pins and is adjustable to a variety of thicknesses? So I made this jig. From the first joint I cut using it, I got airtight joints. It was very cool.

This jig uses a 9° cutting angle. Woodworking books say that 9° is intended more for softwoods than hardwoods (which use a 7° angle) but I thought it a good compromise. You can build this jig entirely by hand, but I cheated and used a table saw for a couple of the precise angle cuts. Let

your conscience be your guide.

One of this jig's peculiarities is that you'll sometimes have to cut right on the pencil line. As designed, this jig works best with Japanese-style ryoba saws on material from ³/₈" to ³/₄" thick. Use the saw's ripping teeth when making your cuts. You could modify this

jig to accommodate Western saws, but you'd have to take a lot of the set out of the teeth so as not to tear up the faces of the jig. The set of a saw's teeth basically allows you to "steer" a blade through a cut. This jig does all the steering. You just have to press the gas.

1 Begin by sandwiching three pieces of wood. This part is made from two pieces of ³⁄₄" × 6" × 36" plywood with a piece of 1" × 1" × 36" solid wood centered between. Use a spacer to index the center precisely in the middle of the larger panels. Glue and nail the sandwich together.

2 Set your saw's blade to 9° and crosscut the end of the sandwich while it's flat on the saw. Next, tilt the blade back to square and set the miter gauge to 9° as shown above. You can use the angled end of the sandwich to set your miter gauge. Lay out a center line down the middle of the sandwich and mark from the end of the line about 3¹⁄₂". Use a sliding T-bevel to transfer the angle to the flat side. This yields a jig that will let you cut dovetails in material as narrow as 3" wide. Any narrower and you'll have to shorten the jig. Lay the extrusion flat on the saw table and cut to the line. The jig will be a little narrower on the other side, but that's OK.

3 Attach the ¹⁄₂" × 4¹⁄₄" × 6" faces to the ends of the jig with nails and glue. Use a ryoba saw to start the cuts to open up the channels in the jig. Use a coping saw to cut out the part of the ends that cover the little channels in the sandwich. Note, the blade is perpendicular to prevent binding on the jig itself. Clean up with a rasp and sandpaper.

4. Lay out and drill 5/16" holes as shown in the diagram. These accommodate the flanged insert nuts for the thumb screws. Attach the flanged inserts using a hex key.

5. Using contact cement, attach 120-grit sandpaper to the same side of the inside channel, on both sides of the jig.

6. Doctor up a couple of 1/4"–20 T-nuts by pounding over the set tines and grinding off a little of the threaded barrels. With some two-part epoxy, attach some 1/8"-thick wooden pads to the face of the T-nuts. When the epoxy is set, sand the pads to fit the T-nuts. Run your thumbscrews through the flanged inserts and attach the T-nut/pads to the thumbscrews with some thread-locking compound (available at any automotive parts store). Finish the jig by attaching something slick to the faces. I used some UHMW (ultra-high molecular weight) plastic self-stick sheeting. It's 1/16" thick, and if you wear out the material on a face, you just peel off the old material and stick on some new. You could just as easily use some wax on the wood faces. You'll just have to sand them flat, eventually.

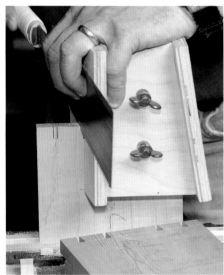

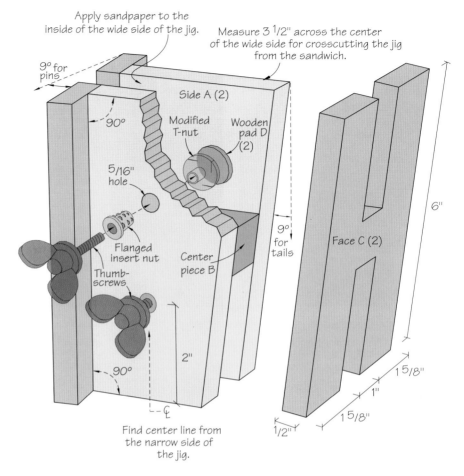

Apply sandpaper to the inside of the wide side of the jig.

Measure 3 1/2" across the center of the wide side for crosscutting the jig from the sandwich.

9° for pins

90°

Side A (2)

5/16" hole

Modified T-nut

Wooden pad D (2)

Flanged insert nut

Center piece B

9° for tails

Face C (2)

Thumb-screws

90°

2"

6"

1 5/8"

1"

1 5/8"

1/2"

Find center line from the narrow side of the jig.

₵

Using the jig couldn't be simpler. I cut tails first. That's a personal choice, but this jig will work well whether you're cutting tails or pins first. The layout is a little simpler than freehand. All you do is mark the depth of the cut with a cutting gauge and lay out the spacing for the tails on the end of the board. Use the pencil marks to cut out the tails, and when you get the waste cleaned out, use the tail end of the board to lay out the pins. Use a sharp pencil for marking, then cut out the pins. Check the fit of the pins to the tails, using a piece of scrap as a hammer block across the whole joint. If they're a little big, do some fitting with a four-in-hand rasp. The joint should be snug, but not so tight that it cracks the tail board when hammering the joint together.

inches (millimeters)

REFERENCE	QUANTITY	PART	STOCK	THICKNESS	(mm)	WIDTH	(mm)	LENGTH	(mm)
A	2	sides	plywood	3/4	(19)	6	(152)	36	(914)
B	1	center piece	poplar	1	(25)	1	(25)	36	(914)
C	2	faces	plywood	1/2	(13)	4 1/4	(108)	6	(152)
D	2	wooden pads		1/8	(3)				

HARDWARE

2	13mm flanged insert nuts	item #32025	Rockler
2	1/4"–20 (6mm–20) thumbscrews		
	3"-wide (76mm-wide) UHMW self-stick tape	item #16L65	Woodcraft
2	1/4"–20 (6mm–20) T-nuts		

Scrap Wood Scraper Plane

This plane helps take the work out of handwork.

BY NICK ENGLER

Once upon a time when I was new to woodworking, someone showed me how to cut my sanding time in half by using a handheld scraper. I thought to myself, "It just doesn't get any better than this."

But it did. A few years later I was introduced to a cabinet scraper — a cast metal frame that holds a scraper at a fixed angle. This reduced my scraping chores considerably, and I thought, "It really can't get any better than this."

But it did. A few more years went by, and someone let me try out their old Stanley scraper plane, an adjustable holder for a scraper. A scraper plane, I quickly learned, is to a cabinet scraper what a Ferrari is to an Astro van. "This," I thought to myself, "is as close to heaven as I am going to get."

And I was right. Scraper planes are not only one of the best smoothing tools ever invented, they are unfortunately as rare as hen's teeth. The old Stanleys are collector's items, and they are priced accordingly. The reproductions that are beginning to appear aren't much less expensive.

Well, if you can't find it or you can't afford it, you can always make it. Not so very long ago, it was common for woodworkers to make their own planes. They aren't particularly difficult tools to make. And the scraper plane, it turns

out, is one of the simplest. In fact, you can make one from scrap wood and a scraper or a worn-out plane iron.

The plane holds a scraper against a wooden support. By turning the adjuster wheels, you can change the angle of the support to compensate for the angle of the burr on the edge of the scraper to get the cut you're after.

Building the Plane

I made this particular scraper plane from some scraps of exotic and figured woods that I just couldn't bring myself to throw away. (Like most woodworkers, I have an overactive pack rat gland.) The sole requires an extremely hard wood to be as durable as possible, so I made that from Cocobolo. But any

Shape the plane handle with a cabinet rasp, rounding over and blending the surfaces until it fits your hand comfortably.

To round the coupling nut, use the pivot to swing it back and forth around the pivot hole as you grind away the end with a sander or grinder.

dense wood will do; rock maple was the traditional planemakers' choice. The other parts are made from curly maple and cherry, but any clear hardwood will work well.

Before you cut the parts, adjust the width of the plane so it's ¹⁄₈" wider than the scraper between the sides. I used the blade from my cabinet scraper, which is 2³⁄₄" wide, making the plane 2⁷⁄₈" wide. I've also made these planes 2¹⁄₈" wide, using 2" plane irons as scraping blades. The plane irons work like gangbusters, by the way.

Because of the loads applied to this tool when you're using it, several of the parts must be reinforced. I drilled a long hole through the back handle and inserted a ³⁄₈"-diameter dowel to prevent it from splitting. I also used dowels to reinforce the ends of the cap bar and the adjuster bar. The cap bars are under considerable tension, and the steel rods will split out of the ends if they are not strengthened. I put dowels in the adjuster bar at right angles to the wood grain because screws do not hold well in end grain.

I also reinforced the joints between the soles and the sides with loose tenons

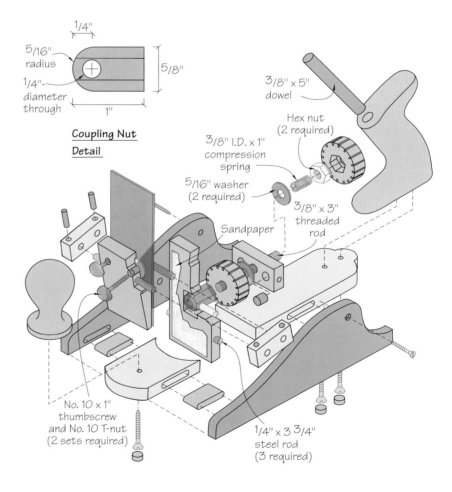

Coupling Nut Detail

1/4"
5/16" radius
1/4"-diameter through
5/8"
1"

3/8" x 5" dowel

Hex nut (2 required)

3/8" I.D. x 1" compression spring

5/16" washer (2 required)

3/8" x 3" threaded rod

Sandpaper

No. 10 x 1" thumbscrew and No. 10 T-nut (2 sets required)

1/4" x 3 3/4" steel rod (3 required)

because cocobolo is an oily wood and does not form an especially strong glue bond. If I had made the soles from rock maple, the tenons would have been unnecessary.

When gluing the sides to the soles, remember that you must put the support, support pivot, coupling nut and coupling nut pivot in position as you do so. The pivot rods are captured by the sides; you cannot insert them after you assemble the plane body.

Using the Scraper Plane

Place the plane on a flat surface. Insert the scraper blade between the support and the cap and slide it down until it touches the surface. Tighten the thumbscrews to lock it in place; I adhere a piece of 100-grit sandpaper to the back of the support to keep the scraper from shifting in use.

Loosen the back adjuster wheel. As you make passes over a piece of wood, turn the front wheel until the blade begins to bite. Then tighten the back wheel and make another pass over the wood. The plane should be resting flat on its sole. If it's not, or you're not getting the cut you want, readjust the vertical position of the blade or the angle of the support. This takes a little futzing around until you get the hang of the tool and how it cuts. Tip: Use a rawhide mallet to tap the blade, making tiny adjustments in the vertical position.

To change the angle of the scraper blade, turn the adjuster wheels. Steeper angles (as the blade approaches vertical) leave a smoother surface; shallow angles remove stock more quickly. To sharpen the scraper blade, grind and file the ends at 30°. Roll the burr with a burnisher. Don't apply too much pressure; a small burr is less likely to grab and leaves a smoother surface than a large burr.

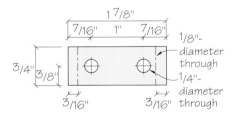

1 7/8"
7/16"   1"   7/16"
3/4" 3/8"
3/16"   3/16"
1/8"-diameter through
1/4"-diameter through

Cap Bar Layout

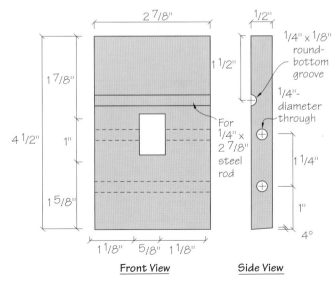

2 7/8"   1/2"
1 7/8"
4 1/2"   1"
1 5/8"
1 1/2"
1/4" x 1/8" round-bottom groove
For 1/4" x 2 7/8" steel rod
1/4"-diameter through
1 1/4"
1"
4°
1 1/8"   5/8"   1 1/8"

Front View   **Side View**

Blade Support Layout

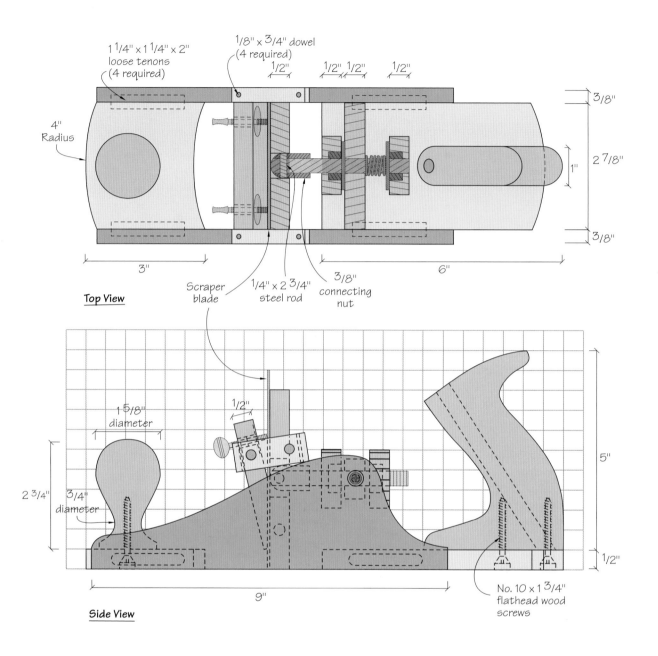

1 1/4" x 1 1/4" x 2"
loose tenons
(4 required)

1/8" x 3/4" dowel
(4 required)

1/2"

1/2" 1/2"

1/2"

3/8"

4"
Radius

2 7/8"

1"

3/8"

3"

6"

Top View

Scraper
blade

1/4" x 2 3/4"
steel rod

3/8"
connecting
nut

1 5/8"
diameter

1/2"

5"

2 3/4"

3/4"
diameter

1/2"

9"

No. 10 x 1 3/4"
flathead wood
screws

Side View

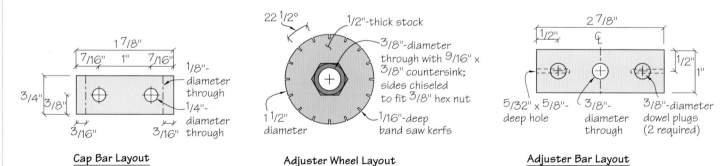

1 7/8"

7/16" 1 7/16"

3/4" 3/8"

1/8"-
diameter
through

1/4"-
diameter
through

3/16" 3/16"

Cap Bar Layout

22 1/2°

1/2"-thick stock

3/8"-diameter
through with 9/16" x
3/8" countersink;
sides chiseled
to fit 3/8" hex nut

1 1/2"
diameter

1/16"-deep
band saw kerfs

Adjuster Wheel Layout

2 7/8"

1/2"

1/2"

1"

5/32" x 5/8"-
deep hole

3/8"-
diameter
through

3/8"-diameter
dowel plugs
(2 required)

Adjuster Bar Layout

Shooting Board

Straighten up your work with this simple jig.

BY JIM STACK

Using a shooting board is a quick and easy way to put a crisp, clean, straight and square edge on stiles, rails and other parts.

The jig is simple to make. Cut out the parts. Be sure that one long edge of the top is straight and smooth. Put that edge on the shelf side of the jig. The plane will rest on the shelf and use this straight edge as a reference when you are planing. Attach the top to the base. Then, attach the stop to the top. Put one screw at one end of the stop, put a square against the stop and square it to the straight edge on the top. Finally, install the bench cleat on the bottom of the base on the opposite end where the stop is located.

Apply wax to the bed and you're ready to start shooting some straight and square edges.

To use the shooting board, let the bench cleat hang over the edge of your bench and let the jig rest on the benchtop. When needed, the removable 45° plate is held in place with a couple of screws.

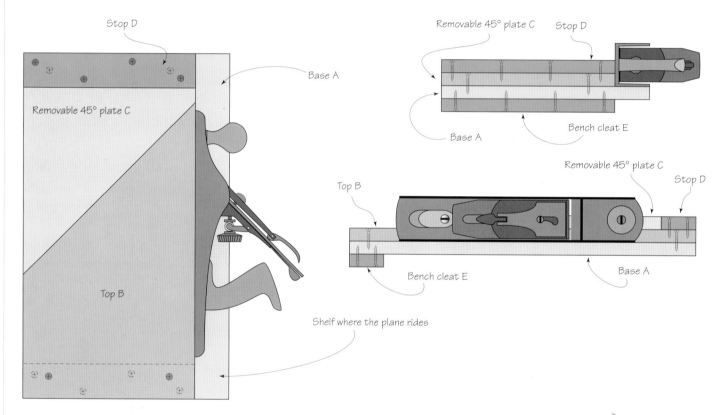

Stop D

Base A

Removable 45° plate C

Top B

Shelf where the plane rides

Removable 45° plate C   Stop D

Base A   Bench cleat E

Top B   Removable 45° plate C   Stop D

Bench cleat E   Base A

inches (millimeters)

REFERENCE	QUANTITY	PART	STOCK	THICKNESS	(mm)	WIDTH	(mm)	LENGTH	(mm)
A	1	base	MDF	3/4	(19)	12	(305)	20	(508)
B	1	top	MDF	3/4	(19)	10	(254)	20	(508)
C	1	removable 45° plate	MDF	3/4	(19)	10	(254)	10	(254)
D	1	stop	MDF	3/4	(19)	2	(51)	10	(254)
E	1	bench cleat	MDF	3/4	(19)	2	(51)	10	(254)

HARDWARE

8   No. 8 × 1¼" (No. 8 × 32mm) flathead wood screws

Very Scary Sharp

A sheet of sandpaper, a slab of marble, a simple jig and wow!

BY NICK ENGLER

Some years ago, Steve LaMantia of Seattle, Washington, posted a long, rambling letter to the Internet news group rec.woodworking (better known as "Wreck Wood") entitled "The D&S Scary Sharp (™) System." Once you waded through Steve's superlatives, exclamations and his stream of consciousness, his message boiled down to just this: You can put a very fine cutting edge on hand tools with sandpaper. That's right — sandpaper.

Other travelers through Wreck Wood spotted Steve's post, tried his methods and posted their own raves. The news spread, sandpaper stock soared and the term *scary sharp* became part of the popular woodworking lexicon. All of which amused those who remember woodworking before there was so much virtual sawdust flying about.

About 40 years ago, I participated in a rite of manhood known as the Boy Scouts of America. There, in the old *Handbook for Boys*, wedged between square knots and Morse code, is this advice: Sharpen your pocketknife with sandpaper.

Well, it was good advice then and better advice now. Continuing developments in abrasives make sandpaper an excellent sharpening material. In many ways, it's easier to use, less expensive to get started with and more versatile than traditional sharpening stones.

Sandpaper — It's Not Just for Sanding Anymore

The most common abrasives in sandpaper are aluminum oxide and silicon carbide, both of which were originally intended to abrade steel. Their application to woodworking was an afterthought. Point of fact — these are the very same abrasives in India stones, grinding wheels, ceramic stones, even Japanese waterstones. Sandpaper is just another form of the abrasive you may already use for sharpening.

The difference is that sandpaper comes in a much wider range of grits than stones and grinding wheels do. Grits between 50 and 2,000 are readily available, and if you look around, you can find sandpaper as coarse as 36 and as fine as 12,000. It's this range that gives sandpaper the edge (pun intended) over other sharpening materials. Traditional stones start between 100 and 200. The finest Arkansas stone is roughly equivalent to 900; the finest ceramic and diamond stones are about 1,200; and the finest waterstone, 8,000 in the Japanese grit system, is close to 2,000 in our American system.

Why is range important? Because proper sharpening technique requires that you hone with progressively finer grits, much like sanding a wooden surface. You can't put a superkeen, scary sharp edge on a tool with just one stone.

Start with coarse abrasives to quickly condition the edge and repair any nicks. This leaves deep scratches in the steel, however, and makes the edge jagged. The chisel is sharper than it was, but not sharp enough. You must continue sharpening with progressively finer abrasives. As you work your way up through the grits, the scratches grow smaller and the edge becomes keener.

Sandpaper not only extends the range from coarse to fine, it gives you more steps in between. If you've ever tried to jump from 80-grit sandpaper to 150-grit when sanding wood, you know how long it can take to work out the scratches left by the coarser grit. It takes less time and you get better results if you work your way up in increments. So it is with sharpening.

The Secret Formula

Stones have it all over sandpaper in one respect: They are rigid. To use sandpaper for sharpening, you must mount it to a flat, rigid surface. Steve and those who came after him recommended $1/4$"-thick plate glass, but this isn't rigid enough. It will flex slightly if your workbench isn't dead flat or there is a bit of sawdust under one corner.

Instead, I use a marble slab to back

up the sandpaper. (Talk about rigid!) You can purchase a precision-milled granite block known as a reference plate from a machinist's supplier, or you can take your straightedge to a cooking supply store and find a reasonably flat marble pastry stone (for rolling out pie dough) for a quarter of the cost. I have a 20"-square pastry stone that mounts eight different sandpaper grits — four on each side.

You can use ordinary sandpaper and stick it to the marble with a spray adhesive; this yields good results. However, I prefer self-adhesive 8"-diameter sanding discs. Because these are made for machine sanding, they have an "open coat" — 40 percent less abrasive on the surface. They cut a little slower, but they last much longer. The open coat prevents the metal filings (the swarf) from becoming impacted between the grits and "loading" the paper. I also look for stearate-impregnated paper; this, too, reduces loading.

For most sharpening tasks, I work my way through four grits — 120, 300, 600 and 1,500. I keep these all on one side of the pastry stone. On the other side, I have 50, 100, 220 and

In addition to chisels, the guide will accommodate gouges, plane irons, skews and parting tools.

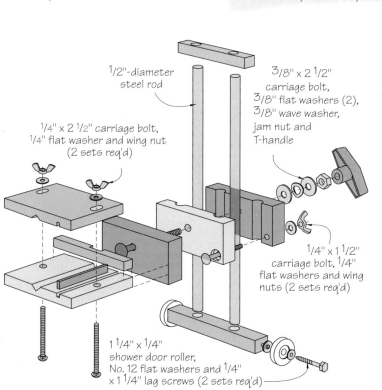

1/2"-diameter steel rod

1/4" x 2 1/2" carriage bolt, 1/4" flat washer and wing nut (2 sets req'd)

3/8" x 2 1/2" carriage bolt, 3/8" flat washers (2), 3/8" wave washer, jam nut and T-handle

1/4" x 1 1/2" carriage bolt, 1/4" flat washers and wing nuts (2 sets req'd)

1 1/4" x 1/4" shower door roller, No. 12 flat washers and 1/4" x 1 1/4" lag screws (2 sets req'd)

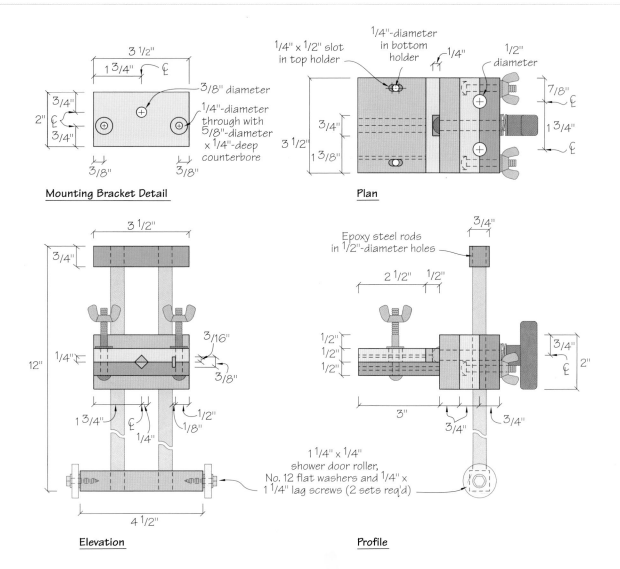

Mounting Bracket Detail

3 1/2"
1 3/4"
℄
3/8" diameter
1/4"-diameter through with 5/8"-diameter x 1/4"-deep counterbore
3/4"
2"
℄
3/4"
3/8" 3/8"

Plan

1/4" x 1/2" slot in top holder
1/4"-diameter in bottom holder
1/4"
1/2" diameter
3 1/2"
3/4"
1 3/8"
7/8"
℄
1 3/4"
℄

Elevation

3 1/2"
3/4"
3/16"
3/8"
12"
1/4"
1 3/4"
℄
1/4"
1/8"
1/2"
4 1/2"

Profile

Epoxy steel rods in 1/2"-diameter holes
3/4"
2 1/2" 1/2"
1/2"
1/2"
1/2"
3"
3/4" 3/4"
3/4"
2"
℄
1 1/4" x 1/4" shower door roller, No. 12 flat washers and 1/4" x 1 1/4" lag screws (2 sets req'd)

2,400. The two coarse grits are to recondition badly damaged edges. The 220 provides an intermediate step between 120 and 300 when I'm flattening the backs of large chisels and plane irons. And the superfine 2,400 is the last step when I'm flattening something.

As you sharpen, brush away the swarf frequently. I use the stiff bristles on the back of a file card. This keeps the abrasive clean and helps prevent loading.

The last step in my sharpening process is stropping. This is the secret ingredient in every successful sharpening formula, no matter what abrasive material you use. Stropping removes tiny burrs and refines the cutting edge, making it as keen as it can possibly get.

For this step, I've mounted a piece of leather to a hard maple board and "charged" it with chromium oxide, a polishing compound. (You might also use jewelers' rouge or tripoli.) Why not mount the leather to the pastry stone? Leather is considerably thicker than the sandpaper. Because of the type of honing guide I use to maintain the sharpening angle, it's important that the stropping surface be at the same level as the other abrasives. I've planed the wood to adjust for the thickness of the leather.

The Secret Weapon — The Very Scary Honing Guide

Yes, I use a honing guide. I know that some experienced sharpeners look down on these jigs as "training wheels," but I don't. If the first secret to successful sharpening is to hone with progressively finer grits, the second secret is to maintain a precise cutting angle as you do so. And you can be much more precise with a guide. After all, if our hands were all that good at maintaining an angle, we wouldn't need planes to hold plane irons.

One of the reasons some folks don't like honing guides is that the current commercial crop is difficult to adjust and not especially versatile. The homemade jig that I've developed holds a chisel by its handle rather than the blade. Because the jig makes a large triangle with the abrasive surface and the tool, it's easier to adjust and maintain the sharpening angle.

The tool holder conforms to every chisel handle that I've been able to find, and it's wide enough to accommodate an iron from a jointer plane. Additionally, the holder pivots, and it can be locked in place or adjusted to roll around an axis. This makes it possible to sharpen not only chisels and plane irons, but also gouges, skews and parting tools.

The basic scary sharp system consists of a selection of sandpapers and a rigid backing plate. I add a stiff brush and a honing guide.

To adjust the holder to rotate, snug the jam nut against the washers, but don't collapse the wave washer. Hold the jam nut from turning with an open-end wrench and tighten the T-handle against it.

After honing, strop your tools on a piece of leather charged with a superfine abrasive polishing compound. If leather is hard to come by, a couple of pieces of typewriter paper adhered to a rigid surface work just as well.

The tool holder mounts to two grooved brackets that slide along steel rods. To adjust the angle at which the guide holds the tool, slide the brackets up or down on the rods and tighten the wing nuts that lock them in place. To secure the holder, rotate it to the desired angle and tighten the T-handle. To adjust the holder so it will roll as you sharpen a gouge, insert a jam nut between the T-handle and the washers. Tighten the jam nut until it just begins to compress the wave washer. Hold the jam nut from turning and tighten the T-handle against it.

As shown, this honing guide will accommodate hand tools up to 18" long. For longer tools, extend the steel rods.

Drill Press Table

Turn your metalworking drill press table into a woodworking table in just a few hours and with only a few dollars' worth of materials.

BY DAVID THIEL

Despite the fact that your drill press is designed mostly for poking holes in sheet metal, it has many uses in a woodshop. It's a mortiser, it's a spindle sander, it bores huge holes and — of course — it drills holes at perfect right angles to the table. Because the table on most drill presses is designed for metalworking, it's hardly suited for these tasks. So I built this add-on table with features that will turn your drill press into a far friendlier machine:

• A fence that slides forward and backward as well as left and right on either side of the drill press's column. This last feature also uses the drill press's tilting table feature with the auxiliary table for angled drilling.

• Built-in stops (both left and right) that attach to the fence for procedures that need to be replicated, such as doweling or chain-drilling mortises.

• Hold-downs that can be used on the fence or on the table for any procedure.

The sizes given in the cutting list are for a 14" drill press, with the center falling 9" from the rear edge of the table and with a 2" notch in the back to straddle the column. Adjust the center location and overall size of the table to match your particular machine.

Build the Base

The base platform for the table is made from ³/₄" plywood, which should be void-free. Again, adjust the size as necessary to fit your drill press. First, you need to get the table ready for the T-slot track, which is what holds the fence and hold-downs in place. Start by locating the four recessed holes that allow the T-slot mechanism to slip into the track without disassembling the mechanism. Each hole is 1¹/₂" in diameter and ³/₈" deep.

Next, locate the grooves in the center of the holes and use a router with a ³/₄"-wide straight bit to cut the grooves to a ³/₈" depth. The T-slot track should fit into the grooves with the top surface just below that of the plywood table. The grooves should be as parallel as possible to one another to allow smooth movement of the fence.

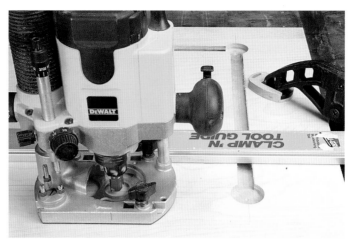

The grooves for the T-slot track allow the fence to be used left to right and front to back on the table to take advantage of the tilting feature of the existing table.

After cutting the hole with a jigsaw, rabbet the opening, using a bearing-piloted router bit. Then chisel the corners square and fit the replaceable insert plate tightly into the rabbet. Make a couple of extra insert plates.

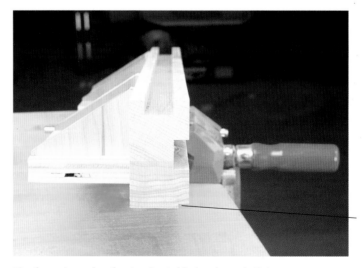

RABBET FOR DUST AND CHIP CLEARANCE

The fence is made of a sturdy, stable hardwood. Cut a groove the length of the top and face of the fence. The grooves hold T-slot tracks, which can be used for stops, hold-downs and other accessories.

Now cut the hole for the 4" × 4" replaceable insert plate. First mark its location on your table, then mark in from that line by $3/8$" to locate your cutting line. Drill clearance holes in two corners of the inner square, then use a jigsaw to cut out the center piece. Next, determine the thickness of the material you will use for your insert plate (the $3/8$"-thick Baltic birch we used is actually metric and shy of $3/8$"). We used a $3/8$" piloted rabbeting bit in a router set to a height to hold the insert flush to the top surface of the table.

While your jigsaw is still out, locate, mark and cut out the notch in the back of the table. This allows the table to move closer to the drill press's post and also to tilt without interference.

As a final friendly touch on the table, I used a $3/8$" roundover bit in my router to soften all the edges on the table, both top and bottom. You'll get fewer splinters if you do this.

A Flexible Fence

The fence is the heart of the table, and the wood should be chosen for durability and straightness. Quarter-sawn hardwood, carefully surfaced and planed, will do nicely. After cutting the fence to size, use a dado stack to mill two $3/8$"-deep by $3/4$"-wide grooves in the fence. The first is centered on the top surface of the fence, and as in the grooves in the base platform, a piece of T-slot track should be used to confirm that the groove is deep enough to allow the track to fit just below the surface of the wood. The second groove is then cut, centered on the face of the fence.

One other bit of table saw work is a $1/8$" by $1/4$"-wide rabbet on the inside bottom edge of the fence. The rabbet keeps debris away from the fence, so your work will fit tightly against it.

One option that I considered was adding an indexing tape measure on the fence. Every time the table is moved, however, the tape would need to be readjusted to zero, and for the infrequent use the tape would see, I decided against it. A stick-on tape can easily be added to the fence face if that's more to your personal taste and needs.

Unlike the fence on a router table,

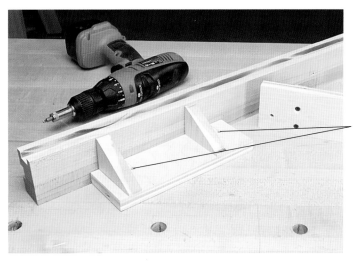

T-SLOT HOLD-DOWNS IN TWO LOCATIONS FOR POSITIONING FENCE

The fence is supported by two simple brackets screwed to the rear of the fence. The location of the triangular braces is important to the track orientation, so follow the diagrams carefully.

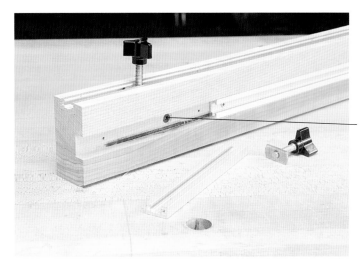

BRACE ATTACHMENT

Install the T-slot tracks in the grooves with flathead screws countersunk into the track. The braces are attached to the fence by screwing through the face groove prior to attaching the T-slot track.

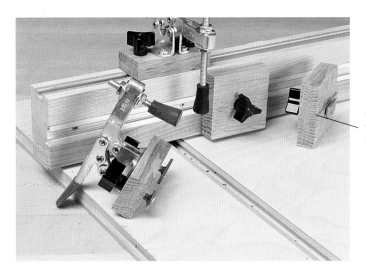

T-SLOT GUIDE HOLDS THE STOPS SQUARELY ON THE FENCE.

The hold-downs and stops are made from $3/4$" hardwood. To make the guide that holds the stops squarely on the fence, cut a $1/16$" by $1 1/8$" rabbet on both sides of the inside face, using your table saw.

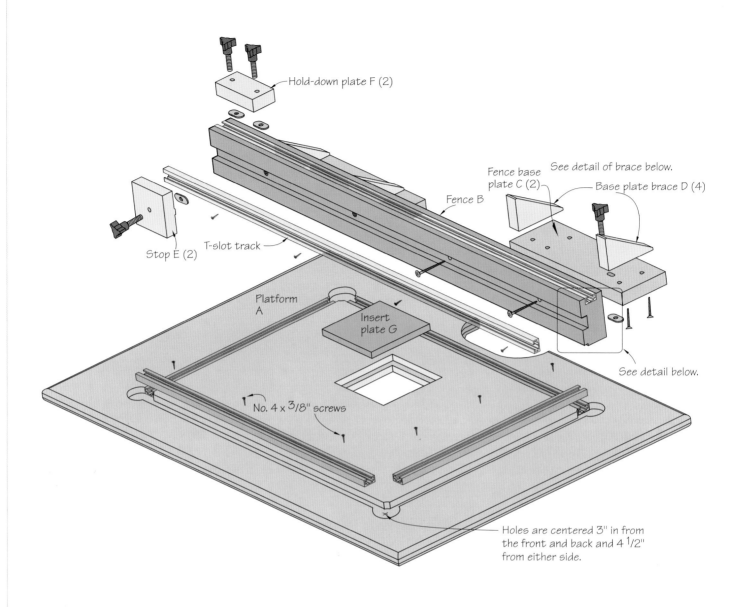

Hold-down plate F (2)

Fence base plate C (2)

See detail of brace below.

Base plate brace D (4)

Fence B

T-slot track

Stop E (2)

Platform A

Insert plate G

No. 4 x 3/8" screws

See detail below.

Holes are centered 3" in from the front and back and 4 1/2" from either side.

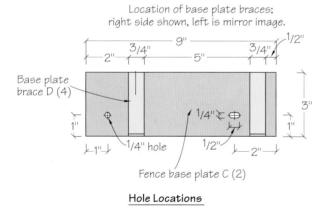

Location of base plate braces; right side shown, left is mirror image.

9"

2" 3/4" 5" 3/4" 1/2"

Base plate brace D (4)

3"

1/4"

1" 1"

1/4" hole 1/2" 2"

Fence base plate C (2)

Hole Locations

Plan Detail of Hole Locations for Base Plate

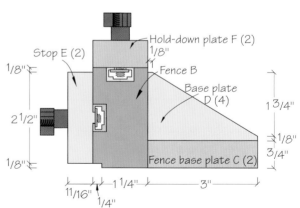

Stop E (2)

Hold-down plate F (2)

1/8"

Fence B

1/8"

Base plate D (4)

2 1/2"

1 3/4"

1/8"

3/4"

Fence base plate C (2)

1/8"

11/16" 1 1/4" 3"

1/4"

Detail of Fence Profile

inches (millimeters)

REFERENCE	QUANTITY	PART	STOCK	THICKNESS	(mm)	WIDTH	(mm)	LENGTH	(mm)
A	1	platform	plywood	3/4	(19)	20	(508)	29	(737)
B	1	fence	hardwood	1 1/2	(38)	2 3/4	(70)	30	(762)
C	2	fence base plates	plywood	3/4	(19)	3	(76)	9	(229)
D	4	base plate braces	hardwood	3/4	(19)	3	(76)	1 7/8	(47)
E	2	stops	hardwood	3/4	(19)	2 1/2	(64)	2 1/2	(64)
F	2	hold-down plates	hardwood	3/4	(19)	1 1/2	(38)	3	(76)
G	1	insert plate	plywood	3/8	(10)	4	(102)	4	(102)

HARDWARE

2	vertical De-Sta-Co clamps	item #88F05.02	Lee Valley
2	1/4"–36 (6mm–36) all-thread plunger		
6	24" (610mm) T-slot tracks	item #12K79.01	Lee Valley
8	1 1/8" (28mm) three-wing knobs	item #00M51.02	Lee Valley
8	T-slot nuts	item #05J21.15	Lee Valley
16	No. 4 × 3/8" (No. 4 × 10mm) flathead screws		
4	lag bolts		

the fence on a drill press table won't see a lot of lateral pressure, so the main purpose of the braces is to hold the fence square to the table at the drilling point. In my case I've also given the braces the job of mounting the fence to the table.

Start by cutting the two base plates and the four braces to size. The braces are triangles with the bottom edge 3" long and the adjoining right angle edge 1 7/8" long. The third side is determined by simply connecting the corners. Locate the braces on the base plates according to the diagrams and predrill and countersink 3/16"-diameter holes in the base plates to attach the braces to the plates.

To mount the support braces to the fence, again refer to the diagrams to locate the proper spacing on the fence. Then drill and countersink screw holes through the face groove in the fence. Clamp the brace to the fence and screw the brace in place.

With the braces attached to the fence, use the T-slot fastener locations on the diagrams as a starting point for drilling the holes in the base plates, but check the location against your table for the best fit. Two holes are drilled in each plate to allow the fence to be moved to the perpendicular position (either to the right or left of the quill), by simply relocating one of the T-slot fasteners. Check each hole in relationship to that position.

Add the Track

Assuming you purchased the 24" lengths of track listed in the hardware list, you should be able to cut the tracks for the table first, leaving falloff that can be added to the two remaining full-length tracks to give you the necessary 30" lengths of track for the fence. When attaching the track, first drill a pilot hole in the center of the track (a groove is provided in the track to simplify that operation), then use a countersink to widen the hole to accommodate a No. 4 × 3/8" flathead screw. Keeping the screw heads flush to the inner surface of the track will make the stops and hold-downs move much easier.

Stops and hold-downs designed for use in T-slot tracks make the drill press most useful. The stops are square blocks of wood with one face milled to leave an indexing strip that fits into the slot on the T-slot track. By using the saw to cut tall but shallow rabbets on two edges of each block, you can complete the stops fairly easily. For safety, cut the rabbet on a longer 2 1/2"-wide piece of wood, then crosscut the stops afterwards. The T-slot fasteners are simply inserted into a 1/4" hole drilled in the center of each stop block.

The hold-downs are blocks of wood with De-Sta-Co clamps screwed to the top. Each block is drilled for two T-slot fasteners. While the De-Sta-Cos are good for this application, they aren't as versatile as I wanted. I replaced the threaded-rod plunger with a longer all-thread (1/4"–36) plunger to provide maximum benefit from the clamps. The rubber tip of the plunger is important to the function of the clamp, and if you can manage to reuse the existing tip, do so. If not, I found rubber stoppers in a variety of sizes in the local Sears hardware store.

To install the stopper, carefully drill a 1/4"-diameter hole two-thirds of the way into the stopper and then you should be able to screw it to the rod easily.

The table should attach easily to your existing drill press table, using four lag bolts countersunk flush into the surface of the auxiliary table. Once attached, the auxiliary table should give you more support and versatility than the metal one.

Mortising Fixture

Slide your way into clean and accurate mortises with this sled mounted on your drill press.

BY JIM STACK

This fixture incorporates a sliding table on top of a fixed table. The part to be mortised is placed on the sliding table against the adjustable fence and clamped in place. The router bit in the drill press is then lowered and locked in place. The sliding table can then be moved side to side, cutting the mortise. The flipper stop fixes the length of the mortise.

Start by cutting out the bottom, sled, runners and guide strips. Attach the runners to the bottom. Then, cut the UHMW (ultra-high molecular weight) plastic strips to size and install it on the tops and inside edges of the runners.

Attach the sled guide strips to the bottom of the sled. The outsides of the guide strips should fit between the runners on the bottom. Take your time and make the sled slide smoothly, with no side-to-side wobbles.

Cut out the fence parts and assemble them. Using a router mounted under a router table, cut the slots in the fence cleat. Using the fence as a template, mark the locations for the T-nuts, drill for the T-nuts and install them. Cut out the two knobs, drill and shape them and install the carriage bolts. Attach the fence guide blocks on the fence assembly and install the fence. Fine-tune the

Attach the UHMW tape on the top and side of the runners.

Bore three or four holes in a row to create the slot for the nut in the adjustment block.

fit and operation of the fence until it moves smoothly and can be locked into place with the knobs.

Now, cut out the two adjustment blocks and drill them for the nuts and bolts. Install the nuts in the side slots. Put the other nuts and washers on the $3\frac{1}{2}$" carriage bolts and install the bolts in the adjustment blocks on the front edge of the sled, approximately 6" apart.

Cut out the two flipper holder blocks and the flipper. Shape these parts as shown in the illustration. Drill the blocks and flipper to accept the wooden dowel. Glue this block/flipper assembly to the center, front edge of the bottom. When clamping this assembly in place, squeeze the two blocks together to hold the flipper in place. Be sure no glue gets on the flipper block. The flipper block should be somewhat stiff to move up and down.

When all is fitted and working smoothly, attach the bottom to your drill press table. Before you start cutting a mortise, be sure the mortise routing bit, the drill press table and the part to be mortised are all securely fastened.

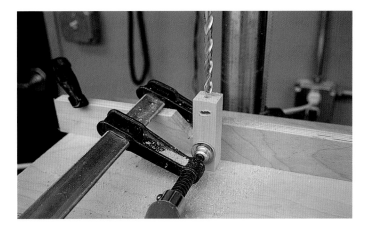

To ensure the hole for the bolt is perfectly straight in the adjustment block, use a drill press.

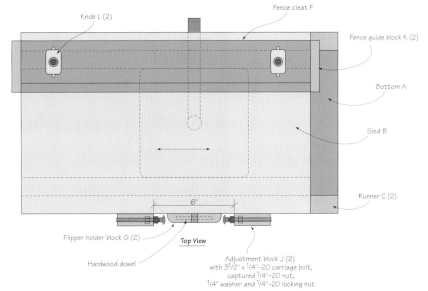

Knob L (2)

Fence cleat F

Fence guide block K (2)

Bottom A

Sled B

Runner C (2)

6"

Flipper holder block G (2)

Top View

Hardwood dowel

Adjustment block J (2) with $3\frac{1}{2}$" x $\frac{1}{4}$"–20 carriage bolt, captured $\frac{1}{4}$"–20 nut, $\frac{1}{4}$" washer and $\frac{1}{4}$"–20 locking nut

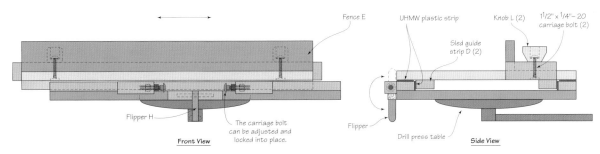

Fence E

UHMW plastic strip

Sled guide strip D (2)

Knob L (2)

$1\frac{1}{2}$" x $\frac{1}{4}$"–20 carriage bolt (2)

Flipper H

The carriage bolt can be adjusted and locked into place.

Front View

Flipper

Drill press table

Side View

inches (millimeters)

REFERENCE	QUANTITY	PART	STOCK	THICKNESS	(mm)	WIDTH	(mm)	LENGTH	(mm)
A	1	bottom	plywood	$\frac{3}{4}$	(19)	15	(381)	24	(610)
B	1	sled	plywood	$\frac{3}{4}$	(19)	15	(381)	24	(610)
C	2	runners	plywood	$\frac{3}{4}$	(19)	$1\frac{1}{2}$	(38)	24	(610)
D	2	sled guide strips	plywood	$\frac{3}{4}$	(19)	$1\frac{1}{2}$	(38)	24	(610)
E	1	fence	plywood	$\frac{3}{4}$	(19)	$2\frac{1}{2}$	(64)	24	(610)
F	1	fence cleat	plywood	$\frac{3}{4}$	(19)	3	(76)	24	(610)
G	2	flipper holder blocks	hardwood	$\frac{3}{4}$	(19)	$\frac{3}{4}$	(19)	$2\frac{1}{4}$	(57)
H	1	flipper	hardwood	$\frac{1}{2}$	(13)	$\frac{11}{16}$	(18)	$2\frac{1}{2}$	(64)
J	2	adjustment blocks	hardwood	1	(25)	1	(25)	3	(76)
K	2	fence guide blocks	hardwood	$1\frac{1}{4}$	(32)	$1\frac{1}{4}$	(32)	2	(51)
L	2	knobs	plywood	$\frac{3}{4}$	(19)	$1\frac{1}{2}$	(38)	$4\frac{1}{4}$	(108)

HARDWARE

21 No. 8 × $1\frac{1}{4}$" (No. 8 × 32mm) flathead wood screws

2 $3\frac{1}{2}$" × $\frac{1}{4}$"–20 (82 × 6mm–20) carriage bolts

2 $\frac{1}{4}$"–20 (6mm–20) nuts

2 $\frac{1}{4}$" (6mm) flat washers

2 $1\frac{1}{2}$" × $\frac{1}{4}$"–20 (38mm x 6mm–20) carriage bolts

2 $\frac{1}{4}$"–20 (6mm–20) T-nuts

1 $\frac{1}{4}$" × 3"-diameter (6mm × 76mm-diameter) dowel

2 UHMW plastic strips

Tilting Table for the Drill Press

Sometimes you need a different angle of approach to your work.

BY JIM STACK

There are times when you need a tilting table on your drill press. This table can be used flat for most boring operations but has the capability of being tilted to any angle in seconds. The fence and stop make it easy to square your work to the drill bit.

Cut the parts as shown in the materials list. Make the fence assembly and cut the two slots in the fence cleat, using a router in a router table. Attach the continuous hinge to the top and bottom parts. Set the fence assembly in place on the top and use it as a template to mark the locations of the hanger bolts. Install the hanger bolts in the top of the top and in the front and back edges of the top. Attach the grooved, metal straps to the front and back edges of the bottom. Install the knobs on the hanger bolts.

Cut the grooves in the fence, using a router mounted in a router table. Using a miter gauge helps to hold the part steady.

Set the fence in place and use it as a template to mark the locations for the hanger bolts.

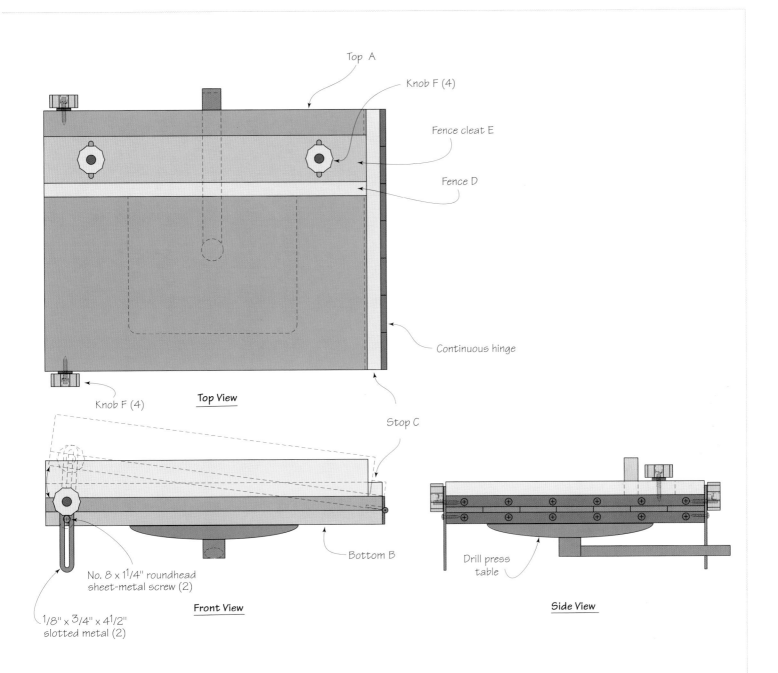

Top A

Knob F (4)

Fence cleat E

Fence D

Continuous hinge

Top View

Knob F (4)

Stop C

No. 8 x 1¹/4" roundhead
sheet-metal screw (2)

Bottom B

Drill press
table

¹/8" x ³/4" x 4¹/2"
slotted metal (2)

Front View

Side View

inches (millimeters)

REFERENCE	QUANTITY	PART	STOCK	THICKNESS	(mm)	WIDTH	(mm)	LENGTH	(mm)
A	1	top	plywood	³/4	(19)	14	(356)	24	(610)
B	1	bottom	plywood	³/4	(19)	14	(356)	24	(610)
C	1	stop	hardwood	³/4	(19)	³/4	(19)	14	(356)
D	1	fence	plywood	³/4	(19)	2¹/4	(57)	23	(584)
E	1	fence cleat	plywood	³/4	(19)	3	(76)	23	(584)
F	4	knobs	plywood	³/4	(19)	2¹/4 dia	(57)		

HARDWARE

1 1¹/4" × 14" (32mm × 356mm) continuous hinge

2 ¹/8" × ³/4" × 4¹/2" (3mm × 19mm × 114mm) metal straps
   with ¹/4"-wide (6mm-wide) slots

4 No. 8 × 1¹/4" (No. 8 × 32mm) roundhead sheet-metal screws

4 1¹/2" × ¹/4"–20 (38mm × 6mm–20) hanger bolts

4 ¹/4"–20 (6mm–20) T-nuts

4 ¹/4"(6mm) fender washers

Auxiliary Band Saw Table

The cure for the incredible shrinking work surface isn't a new band saw.

BY NICK ENGLER

There I was, perfectly content with my minuscule 14"-square band saw table, not even aware that there was something far, far better. Then I took a job teaching wood craftsmanship at the University of Cincinnati, and life was never the same. I walked into class and was smitten by a classic Tannewitz band saw. This industrial-size baby had 20" wheels, more cast iron than an armory and, best of all, a table that was bigger than most workshops. I was seduced by the ease with which you could handle workpieces of all sizes on that expansive surface.

If you've never worked on a large band saw, you'd be surprised and delighted by how it supports and balances the work. It also adds to the safety and accuracy of operations that involve large boards. If you use your band saw for ripping and resawing, the large table mounts a longer fence, making those chores easier.

No longer satisfied with a small work surface, I studied my own band saw and was amazed to find it has room for a much larger table. Fact is, almost all band saws that are made for small workshops will accommodate bigger tables. In most cases you can easily triple the size of your work surface. I expanded my table from 196" square to 576" square!

To expand the work surface on a band saw, make an auxiliary table. The simplest way to do this is to cut a piece of plywood or particleboard to the size you want. Drill a hole for the blade no more than 10" from the front edge. Cut a saw kerf from an outside edge to the hole. Attach this fixture to the saw by bolting it to the fence rails, if your machine has them. If not, fashion wooden clamps to hook over the bottom edge of the metal table and screw them to the underside of the auxiliary table.

While this design works well, it has a drawback. It decreases the vertical capacity of the saw by the thickness of the auxiliary table. You'll find yourself

The tie bar holds the auxiliary table rigid after allowing space for the fixture to be slipped over the blade. Use a wooden clamp to hold the fixture's surface flat while you tighten the tie bar.

The expansive surface of the band saw table gives you extra support when you need it, such as when cutting large ovals.

removing the fixture when sawing thick stock or resawing wide boards — the very occasions when an expanded table is most needed.

To solve this problem, I made the auxiliary band saw table you see here to extend the existing table, rather than cover it. The extension is made from medium-density fiberboard (MDF) and edged with hardwood. I covered the surfaces with plastic laminate to make them more durable, although this isn't absolutely necessary. The cutout in the middle of the extension is made to the same size and shape as the band saw's table, so the extension rests on the old fence rails. If your band saw doesn't have rails, bolt hardwood cleats to the edges. Rabbet the extension so the top surface will be flush with the table. I cut my rabbets a little deeper than they needed to be, then shimmed the extension with strips of masking tape to get it dead even with the table. Secure the extension by bolting it to the rails (or cleats).

You can make this extension any size you want, but don't extend the table more than 4" at the front. Any more, and it may become difficult to reach the blade while you're working. Don't make the table rectangular; knock off the corners to prevent painful bumps and scrapes. To mount a fence and other jigs, rout slots in the extension at the front and the back.

I've gotten so fond of this extended work surface that I can't imagine how I ever did without it. It's not exactly a Tannewitz, but it's the next best thing.

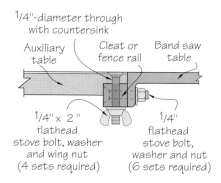

1/4"-diameter through with countersink

Auxiliary table

Cleat or fence rail

Band saw table

1/4" x 2 " flathead stove bolt, washer and wing nut (4 sets required)

1/4" flathead stove bolt, washer and nut (6 sets required)

Mounting Detail

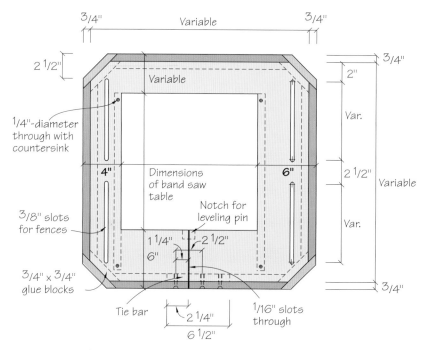

3/4" Variable 3/4"

2 1/2"

Variable

3/4"

2"

Var.

1/4"-diameter through with countersink

4"

6"

Dimensions of band saw table

Notch for leveling pin

2 1/2"

Variable

Var.

3/8" slots for fences

1 1/4"

6"

2 1/2"

3/4" x 3/4" glue blocks

3/4"

Tie bar

2 1/4"

6 1/2"

1/16" slots through

Top View

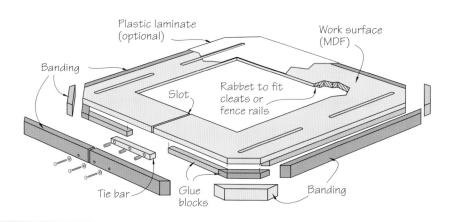

Plastic laminate (optional)

Work surface (MDF)

Banding

Slot

Rabbet to fit cleats or fence rails

Tie bar

Glue blocks

Banding

Band-Sawn Pencil Posts

Don't have a jointer or a router? Here's another way to build eight-sided tapering posts.

BY NICK ENGLER

One of the axioms of wood-working is that there are always at least three good ways to accomplish any one task. This, in fact, was the premise of a book by a good friend of mine, Bob Moran, author of *Woodworking: The Right Technique* (Reader's Digest, 2001). Bob proves this old saw by showing the reader three ways to accomplish dozens of common woodworking chores. The healthy sales of his book also prove that woodworkers tend to collect these techniques the way cooks collect recipes.

When the folks at *Popular Woodworking* told me they were planning a project on a pencil-post bed, I said, "I've got a nifty jig for making pencil posts." And, sure enough, my technique was different from the one that Troy Sexton used to make his bed. Not better, just different. So for those technique collectors among you, here's another pencil-post recipe for your files.

Begin by tapering the faces of the stock. As you cut, make sure the bottom of the post is butted against the end of the jig. Wedges hold the post in position at the top of the jig.

93

Pencil-Post Jig

My particular technique relies on a tapering jig — a very long tapering jig designed to be used on the band saw. This jig holds the pencil-post stock at a slight angle to the blade — 0.83° in the example shown. The top of the post is held by a dowel so the post stock can pivot. The bottom portion of the stock is cradled in special holders. These holders index the stock so you can turn it precisely 45° between cuts.

As shown in these drawings, the jig will help to create a pencil post that's 82" long and 2½" square. However, the design can be adapted easily to make posts of any size. First, rip the side and base of the jig from the long edges of a sheet of ¾"-thick plywood; the factory edges will be relatively straight. Stack the holder parts face-to-face and cut two identical holders. Drill the hole in one end and assemble the parts, except for the dowel pivot and the middle holder.

You want to leave the dowel loose so you can mount the stock in the jig and take it out again. To position the middle holder, mount a post in the jig and place the holder under it. Slide the holder along the post until it's 30" from the bottom end. Mark the position of the holder on the base, then attach it with screws. Don't worry that one end of the middle holder hangs over the edge of the base. You'll cut this off when you make your first pass on the band saw.

Making a Band-Sawn Pencil Post

To mount the post stock in the jig, you must drill a ½"-diameter hole in the top end. (After making the post, you can use this same hole to attach the finial if you have one.) Mount the post stock in the jig and turn it so one of the faces is parallel to the band saw blade. Mount a fence on the band saw and position it so the distance from the fence to the blade is equal to the width of the jig.

Slowly feed the jig and the stock past the blade, keeping the back of the jig firmly against the band saw's fence. Cut tapers in the faces of the stock, turning the stock 90° between each cut. The blade should exit the stock at the middle

holder, 30" from the bottom end of the stock. When you've finished this step, you should have a four-sided taper.

If you were to continue cutting the corner tapers in this manner, they would exit near the bottom of the post. This is because the post is wider when measured diagonally than it is when measured across the face. To stop the corner tapers at the same point as the face tapers, you will need to cut transition curves in the corners.

To figure the radius (R) of these curves, subtract the stock's width (W) from the diagonal measurement (D). Then subtract the result from the width and divide by two. The equation looks like this: $[W - (D - W)]/2 = R$.

For example, if you're making a pencil post 2½" wide, the diagonal measurement is $3^{17}/_{32}$". Plug these values into the equation, and you'll

The holder cradles the pencil-post stock and indexes it every 45°, allowing you to cut a perfect octagonal taper on your post.

After cutting the face tapers, mark the transition curves on the corners of the post. I made a simple marking jig to do this quickly and accurately.

Cut the transition curves with a coping saw. Take it slow and monitor the lines on both sides of the cut. Cut on the waste side of the line. Later, you can sand or file the curves to the line to shape them precisely.

find the radius of the transition curve should be 4⁷⁄₆₄". Mark the radius on both sides of each corner, then cut the curves with a coping saw.

Rotate the stock in the jig so the faces are 45° to the blade. Cut the corner tapers, stopping when you reach the transition curves. Between each cut, back the jig out of the saw and rotate the stock 90°.

After cutting the tapers, smooth the sawed surface with a block plane, scraper and sandpaper. Don't cut too deeply when you plane or scrape! You just want to remove the saw marks; you don't want to change the symmetrical shape of the post.

Tip: To get the smoothest surface possible when cutting with your band saw, use a blade with milled teeth. Ordinary band saw blades are stamped and set, but most woodworking suppliers carry a better brand of milled blade. They cost about twice as much as an ordinary blade, but they save an enormous amount of work when you need an accurate cut and a smooth surface.

Cut the corner tapers up to the transition curves. Be careful not to cut past the curves; stop the moment the waste falls away and back the stock out of the saw.

Plane and scrape the sawn surfaces just enough to remove the saw marks. The pencil-post jig holds the post for this operation; just clamp the base to your bench.

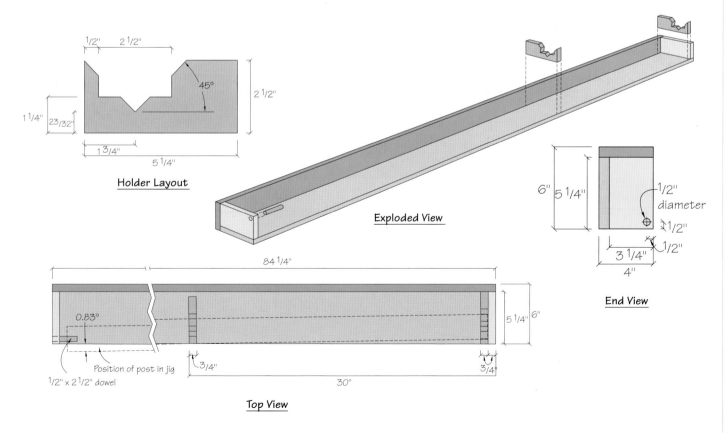

Holder Layout

1/2"   2 1/2"
45°
2 1/2"
1 1/4"   23/32"
1 3/4"
5 1/4"

Exploded View

6"   5 1/4"   1/2" diameter
1/2"
3 1/4"   1/2"
4"

End View

84 1/4"

0.83°
Position of post in jig
1/2" x 2 1/2" dowel
3/4"
30"
3/4"
5 1/4"   6"

Top View

Circle-Cutting Fixture for the Band Saw

If you've got a penny and some scrap wood, you can make this fixture in 30 minutes.

BY JIM STACK

This fixture uses a sliding dovetail to hold the sliding arm in place. The arm is locked in place using a T-nut, a finger bolt and a penny.

Cut the parts as listed in the cutting bill. Cut the bevels on the top plates and the sliding arm. Set the top plates and the sliding arm on the base. Attach the plates to the base, making sure the arm slides easily between the top plates.

Set the fixture on the band saw and mark the locations of the runner and the bottom cleat. Then, attach the runner and the cleat to the base.

Drill a ¾"-diameter hole in the center of the dovetail groove in the base. Drill this hole deep enough to accept the thickness of the T-nut shoulder and the penny. Then bore the hole for the bolt. Insert the T-nut and seat it in place, put the penny on top of the T-nut, slide the sliding arm in place and insert the finger bolt.

Attach the fixture to the band saw and you're good to go.

Set your table saw blade angle to 10°. Cut the bevel on one long edge of each top plate and both edges of the sliding arm.

Bore the clearance hole for the T-nut's shoulder and the penny. Then bore the hole for the bolt.

To use the fixture, measure from one edge of the blank and mark the radius. Drill a 1/4"-diameter hole just deep enough to accept the pivot pin. Set the blank on the fixture, inserting the pivot pin in the hole in the blank. Move the sliding arm until the edge that you marked is lightly touching the saw blade. Tighten the bolt to hold the arm in place. Turn on the saw and make the cut.

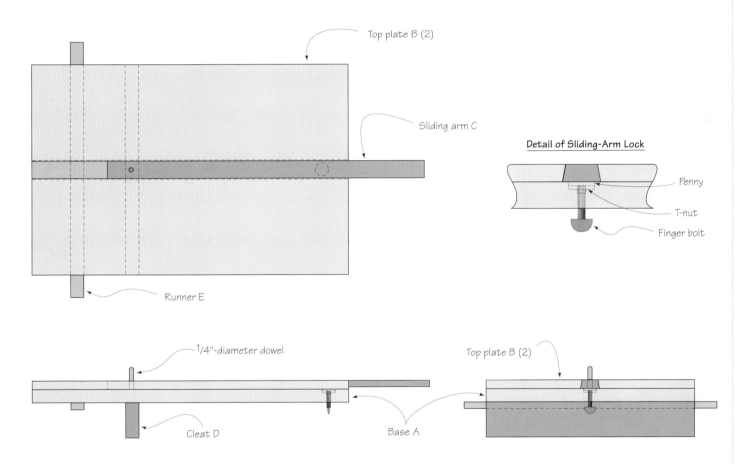

Top plate B (2)

Sliding arm C

Detail of Sliding-Arm Lock

Penny

T-nut

Finger bolt

Runner E

1/4"-diameter dowel

Cleat D

Base A

Top plate B (2)

inches (millimeters)

REFERENCE	QUANTITY	PART	STOCK	THICKNESS	(mm)	WIDTH	(mm)	LENGTH	(mm)
A	1	base	plywood	3/4	(19)	12	(305)	18	(457)
B	2	top plates	plywood	1/2	(13)	5 3/4	(146)	3	(76)
C	1	sliding arm	plywood	1/2	(13)	1 3/8	(35)	18	(457)
D	1	cleat	plywood	3/4	(19)	2	(51)	12	(305)
E	1	runner	hardwood	3/8	(10)	3/4	(19)	15	(381)

HARDWARE

1 1 1/2" × 1/4"–20 (38mm x 6mm–20) finger bolt

1 1/4"–20 (6mm–20) T-nut

1 1/4" × 1" (6mm × 25mm) dowel

1 penny (any minting date will work!)

Ultimate Miter Saw Stand

This stand has all the features you'll ever need to make your miter saw happy.

BY JIM STUARD

When I worked in professional shops, there was always a chop saw on some kind of cart. The less-organized shops put the saw on the nearest work cart. It didn't take up much space, but it wasn't as useful as it should be. The better shops mounted the miter saw to a rolling cart and attached permanent wings to support long pieces and to hold a fence with stops for doing repetitive cuts. This setup was useful, but it took up a lot of space.

What I had in mind for *Popular Woodworking*'s shop would have a dead-on stop system and folding wings so the stand would take up less space. The top of this stand adjusts up and down so you can line up the saw's table with the wings. (In fact, the adjustable table allows you to use a drill press or a mortiser on this stand.) It has onboard dust collection that turns itself on and off. And the kicker to the whole thing is that the cart is made from one sheet each of ³⁄₄" and ¹⁄₂" plywood, with some solid-wood trim.

Begin construction by cutting the parts out according to the cutting list and using the optimization diagram. You'll notice that the case top is in two pieces on the optimization diagram. That's because you have to edge-glue the plywood together, then cut it to size. There isn't much scrap on this project.

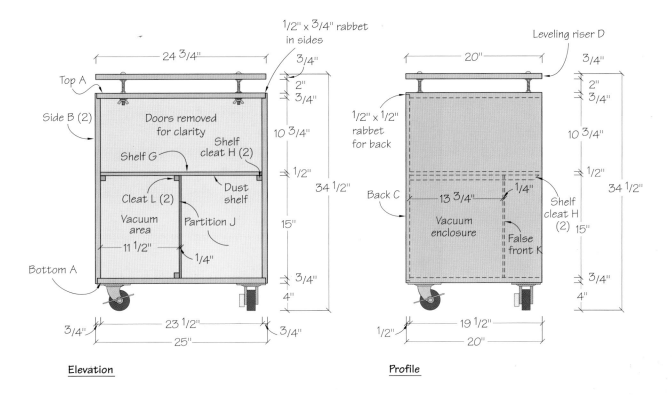

Elevation | **Profile**

One Quick Cabinet

Begin by building the cabinet. To join the sides to the top and bottom, first cut $1/2$" by $3/4$" rabbets in the top and bottom edges of the sides. To hold the back, cut $1/2$" by $1/2$" rabbets in the back edges of the sides, top and bottom pieces. Now assemble the case. An old trade secret is to lay the case facedown on your assembly bench. This way you can ensure the joint at the inside of the rabbet is flush all around. Set each joint with a couple of nails, then screw the case together. Check your cabinet for squareness and make sure the back fits snugly. Attach the back with screws. Flush up the front edges of the cabinet with a plane and apply iron-on birch veneer tape. File the tape flush, sand the cabinet and mount the casters.

An Adjustable Saw Platform

Now is a good time to mount the leveling riser (or platform) to your cabinet and get the miter saw set up. First, cut a $1^{1/2}$" radius on the corners of the riser. Make sure this cut is square so that you can apply veneer tape without too much trouble. Ironing on veneer tape to the riser in one piece is a real challenge, but it looks great.

When the riser is ready, center it on top of the case and clamp it in place. Place your miter saw in the center of the riser. With a pencil, trace the locations of your saw's feet onto the riser. Also trace the holes in the machine's feet that you'll use to mount the saw to the riser. This is important because the riser floats over the case on four bolts, which allows you to adjust the saw up and down. Now mark locations for the bolts that attach the riser to the case. Be sure to keep the bolts as close as you can to the feet without them interfering with each other.

When you've marked the locations for the riser bolts, drill your holes completely through the riser and the top of the case. To minimize tear-out, hold a piece of scrap inside the case where the drill will come out. Now ream out the holes a little to ease the riser adjustment.

Remove the riser from the case and drill the holes for mounting the saw. Now you can mount the riser to the case (see the list of hardware you need). Put the bolt through the fender washer, then into the hole in the riser. Put another flat washer on the other side of the riser with a jam nut to set the bolt in place. Run a jam nut up the bolt, leaving a 2" gap between riser and the loose jam nut. Place wash-ers over the holes in the case and set the riser in place.

On the underside of the case, put a flat washer on the bolt, followed by a lock washer and a wing nut. When you want to adjust the riser height, simply loosen the wing nuts and adjust the jam nut against the case top.

To complete the case, build and hang the plywood doors. Nail a $13/16$" solid-maple edge with a bullnose profile to the edges.

Use European hinges (sometimes called concealed hinges) on your doors. I'm fond of a $30 Euro-Eze jig that easily locates the holes for the hinges and the mounting plates. Drill the hinges' cup holes about 4" in from the top and bottom of the case.

Automatic Vacuum

Now mount the saw and outfit the cabinet with the vacuum and electrical parts. When the saw and vacuum are hooked up properly, the vacuum will come on automatically when you turn the saw on (thanks to the Craftsman auto switch), and it will turn off a few seconds after you finish your cut.

Start by drilling two 2" holes in the back near the bottom of the case. One hole is for the vacuum hose (locate

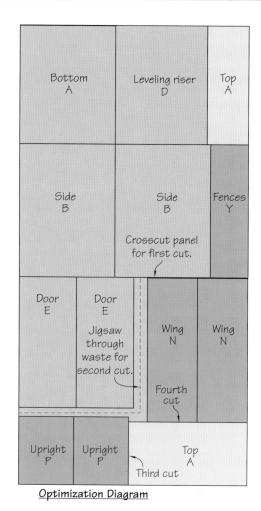

Bottom A	Leveling riser D	Top A
Side B	Side B	Fences Y
	Crosscut panel for first cut.	
Door E	Door E	Wing N
	Jigsaw through waste for second cut.	Wing N
		Fourth cut
Upright P	Upright P	Top A
	Third cut	

Optimization Diagram

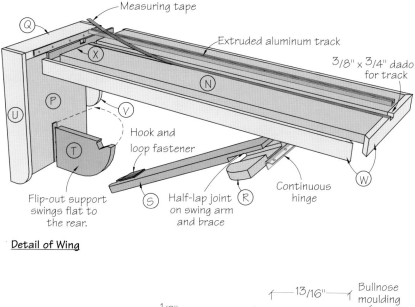

Measuring tape

Extruded aluminum track

3/8" x 3/4" dado for track

Hook and loop fastener

Flip-out support swings flat to the rear.

Half-lap joint on swing arm and brace

Continuous hinge

Detail of Wing

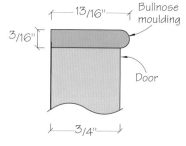

1/4"   30° angle   1/2"

3/4"   ↗1/4"

4 7/8"   4 5/8" radius   1 5/16"

7 3/4"

Flip-Out Support

13/16"   Bullnose moulding

3/16"   Door

3/4"

Detail of Door Trim

it according to your vacuum). The other is for the wiring. I enclosed the vacuum in a partition made from two pieces of plywood and the shelf. The shelf height in the drawing works for the two-gallon Craftsman vacuum. Lay out the height of the bottom edge of the shelf. Mount a pair of cleats to these lines. Screw the shelf in from the top.

Now screw cleats to the inside of the case to make the partition and false front that conceals the vacuum. Notch your plywood pieces to wrap around the shelf cleat and the power cord for the vacuum. Turn the vacuum's switch to "on," place it in the new cubby and hook up the vacuum's hose to the saw through a hole in the back.

Screw an outlet strip to the bottom of the case and run the strip's cord through a hole in the back. Plug the auto switch into the outlet strip and plug in the saw. Now screw the partition and false front in place to conceal the vacuum.

Huge Wings

The wings are the last thing to do. Begin by gluing and nailing 1/4"-thick solid-wood edge trim to one end of the wings. This edging gives the continuous hinge some meat to bite into. Finish the wings by applying the 1/2" by 1 1/2" trim to the other three edges.

Study the diagram to see how the wings are supported. First, apply upright ledges to the uprights. Cut the 2" radii on the brackets and then attach them in place.

Cut the swing arms, braces and flip-out supports. The swing arm and brace need a half-lap joint that makes a T shape. Attach the continuous hinge to the top of the T. The best way to cut this joint is with a dado head in a table saw. Cut a 3/4" by 3/4" notch on the end of the swing arms to mate with the flip-out support.

The last thing to do to the arms is to round off the corners: 1" on the ends and 3 1/2" on the brackets. Now mount

the swing-arm assemblies to the underside of the wings, using a 10" piece of continuous hinge, with the notched end of the swing arm 1/4" in from the point where the wing meets the case. To keep everything from flopping around when the arms are down, use adhesive-backed hook and loop fasteners between the swing arms and wings. Reinforce the adhesive with staples.

Finish the wings by cutting a 3/8" by 3/4" dado down the middle of the wing for the extruded aluminum channel for the stop. Next to that dado, cut a second shallow dado that's 1/2" wide and as deep as your stick-on measuring tape is thick. Cut the aluminum channel to length and screw it in place.

Now concentrate on the flip-out supports. After cutting out the mating notches for the swing arms, cut a 3/16" by 5/8" rabbet into the end of the support to accept a 4 3/4"-long piece of continuous hinge. Lay out and mount the support to the upright, centered

inches (millimeters)

REFERENCE	QUANTITY	PART	STOCK	THICKNESS	(mm)	WIDTH	(mm)	LENGTH	(mm)	
■ CABINETS										
A	2	top & bottom	plywood	3/4	(19)	20	(508)	24¹/2	(623)	
B	2	sides	plywood	3/4	(19)	20	(508)	27³/4	(705)	
C	1	back	plywood	1/2	(13)	24¹/2	(623)	27¹/4	(692)	
D	1	leveling riser	plywood	3/4	(19)	20	(508)	24³/4	(629)	
E	2	doors	plywood	3/4	(19)	12¹/16	(307)	27³/8	(696)	size before applying door trim
F	1	door trim	solid wood	3/16	(5)	13/16	(21)	16'	(4.9m)	
G	1	shelf	plywood	1/2	(13)	19¹/2	(496)	23¹/2	(597)	
H	2	shelf cleats	solid wood	3/4	(19)	3/4	(19)	19	(483)	
J	1	partition	plywood	1/4	(6)	15	(381)	14	(356)	
K	1	false front	plywood	1/4	(6)	15	(381)	11¹/2	(292)	
L	2	cleats	solid wood	3/4	(19)	3/4	(19)	13³/4	(349)	
M	1	cleat	solid wood	3/4	(19)	3/4	(19)	5	(127)	
■ WINGS										
N	2	wings	plywood	3/4	(19)	10³/8	(264)	30	(762)	
P	2	uprights	plywood	3/4	(19)	11¹/2	(292)	14¹/2	(369)	
Q	2	upright ledges	solid wood	3/4	(19)	2³/4	(70)	11¹/2	(292)	
R	2	swing-arm braces	solid wood	3/4	(19)	4	(102)	10¹/2	(267)	
S	2	swing arms	solid wood	3/4	(19)	3	(76)	20	(508)	
T	2	flip-out supports	solid wood	3/4	(19)	4⁷/8	(124)	7³/4	(197)	
U	2	front brackets	solid wood	1/2	(13)	2³/4	(70)	15	(381)	
V	2	rear brackets	solid wood	1/2	(13)	2³/4	(70)	10	(254)	
W	1	wing trim	solid wood	1/2	(13)	1¹/2	(38)	15'	(4.6m)	
X	1	edge trim	solid wood	1/4	(6)	13/16	(21)	24	(610)	
Y	2	fences	plywood	3/4	(19)	3	(76)	16¹/4	(412)	
Z	1	stop block	solid wood	3/4	(19)	2	(51)	3	(76)	

HARDWARE

■ CASE

4   4" (102mm) caster with locking wheels

16   No. 10 × 1/2" (No. 10 × 13mm) pan head sheet metal screws

16   1/4" (6mm) lock washers

1   6-outlet plug strip

  nails

8' (2.5m) iron-on birch veneer tape

■ LEVELING RISER

4   4¹/2" × 3/8" (115mm × 10mm) stove bolts (coarse thread)

4   1/2" × 1¹/2" (13mm x 38mm) fender washers

12   3/8" (10mm) flat washers

4   3/8" (10mm) lock washers

4   3/8" (10mm) wing nuts (coarse thread)

8   3/8" (10mm) jam nuts (coarse thread)

12' (3.75m) iron-on birch veneer tape

■ VACUUM

1   2-gallon Craftsman wet/dry vacuum
item #17711   Sears

1   Craftsman auto switch
item #24031   Sears

■ DOORS

4   130° European-style cup hinges

1   Euro-Eze jig   item #905-599
Woodworker's Supply

■ SAW (fastening to leveling support)

4   2¹/2" × 1/4"–20 (64mm × 6mm–20) hex-head bolts

8   1/4" (6mm) flat washers

4   1/4" (6mm) lock washers

4   1/4"–20 (6mm–20) wing nuts

■ WING SUPPORTS AND FENCE

8   2" × 1/4"–20 (51mm × 6mm–20) hex-head bolts

16   1/4" (6mm) flat washers

8   1/4" (6mm) lock washers

8   1/4"–20 (6mm–20) wing nuts

2   36" (914mm) continuous hinges

3   36" (914mm) T-track   item #128219 Woodcraft

1   72" (1829mm) left-to-right reading tape

1   72" (1829mm) right-to-left reading tape

2   2" (51mm) square sets of hook and loop fasteners

  nails

■ STOP

1   1/4"–20 (6mm–20) star knob

1   1¹/2" × 1/4"–20 (38mm × 6mm–20) hex-head bolt

1   1/4" (6mm) flat washer

and flush to the bottom edge.

The last step on the wings is to attach the wing assembly to the upright. Do this carefully so that the surface of the wing is flush with the upright ledge. Now, if everything's OK, your wings should lock flush and square to the upright. If you didn't get it right the first time, add a flathead screw to the inside of each notch and you will be able to adjust the height of the wing.

To attach the wing assemblies, temporarily remove the saw/riser assembly and remove the wing from the upright assembly. Cut a spacer that's $2^3/4$" plus the height of the saw's table. Clamp the spacer flush to the upright ledge. Lay the wing assembly on the edge of the case. On the saw/riser assembly, measure from the front edge of the riser to the saw fence. Subtract $1^3/4$" from that number and mark it on the case, measuring from the front. This is where the upright should be mounted. It accounts for the thickness of the $3/4$" saw fence and the distance from the center of the stop to the fence. Mount the upright with the hardware listed. Make sure to counterbore the bolt heads and washers. This allows the flip-out support to fold flat against the upright. Reattach the wings and flush the saw table up to the wings by resting a straight piece of lumber across the wings. Adjust the saw's height and lock it down.

The last step is to make the fences and the stop, and to attach the tapes. First, rip a couple of $3^1/2$"-wide sections of plywood from your scrap. Then cut them to 1" longer than the distance from the blade to the outside edge of the upright. That should be about $16^1/4$", as long as your saw is centered correctly on the base.

Cut $3/8$" by $3/4$" dadoes 1" to the center from one edge. The edge that the dado is closest to is the bottom edge. Repeat the $1/2$" dado for the tape so it's above the dado. Glue a 4"-long filler into the groove at the end next to the blade and attach a length of aluminum channel to fill the remaining length. Make a mirror part for the other side. This keeps your hands at least 4" away from the blade — a safe distance. Attach the fences by lowering the saw (as if you were making a cut) and butting each

Adjusting the height of the saw is as easy as loosening the wing nuts inside the cabinet and using the jam nuts on top of the cabinet to raise or lower the saw until it's flush with the two wing assemblies.

The easiest way to assemble the wing is to attach the hinge to the upright assembly. Then remove it and attach it to the wing. Clamp the upright in a vise and reattach everything. Make sure to mark each hinge's location or some parts won't fit together properly.

fence against the blade. Clamp the fence pieces there and screw them in place.

Cut the measuring tape to 16" and stick it in place. Use a square block to index off the 16" marks and, after cutting the tapes to length (around 46"), stick them in place, butting the end up against the block on each side of the saw blade.

Finally, make the stop that runs in the channel. The stop is a simple 2" by 3" block with a $1/4$" hole in it. Make a guide strip that's about $5/16$" by $1/16$". It's easier if you make the strip a little thick and plane it down to the $1/16$" thickness. Drill the $1/4$" hole through and test it with a bolt and star knob.

There is a lot of aluminum channel out there these days, but I chose this T-track because a $\frac{1}{4}$"–20 bolt head will fit in the channel. It comes predrilled and countersunk and machines nicely. You'll probably have to file down some screws that pop out from the other side.

Here you can see how the stop works with the fence system. Note the thin guide strip that prevents your stop from wobbling as you set it.

Blast Gate for a Shop Vacuum

Connect two machines to one vacuum with a time-saving switch that can be built in an afternoon using scraps.

BY JACK BOWLEY

I have a fairly small workshop, and I typically use my shop vacuum to collect sawdust from my band saw and my disc/belt sander — in addition to the shop vacuum's role as a general sawdust steward.

I found that the chore of switching the hose from one machine to the other sometimes caused me to skip dust collection in favor of convenience. I was determined to solve the problem by using available materials, and I have produced the following "vacuum switch." It will instantly redirect the suction from one machine to the other, even without turning off the shop vacuum.

This little unit is easily fabricated from plywood and wood scraps, and it can be put together in an afternoon. The extra plastic vacuum hoses used to connect your machines are easily found, discarded from broken vacuum cleaners, at most thrift shops for a dollar or from your local home-improvement center. And if you must cut a hose in order to shorten it, you can make a new end piece using a 35mm film container with the bottom removed. The lip around the top of the canister will engage the corrugations of most plastic vacuum hoses after it is gently forced into the hose's end. This also forms a swiveling connector to attach to the switch.

The drawings are self-explanatory. Basically the jig is made of a series of layers. Each layer has a hole or holes cut inside it, and each hole is designed to do a specific job. The jig's outside shape is easily cut out on a band saw, and the holes are cut using a band saw (or scroll saw) and drill press. The entire unit is glued and screwed together. Refer to the diagrams for the exact locations of all the holes.

Cut Your Shapes

Use the diagrams to lay out the shapes on all your parts before making any cuts. The drawings are gridded so you can enlarge them to full size using graph paper. The first step is to cut parts B, C, D, E and F. Because these parts share a common outside contour, the rough-cut pieces should be taped together with double-sided tape before cutting them on the band saw and sanding, after which they can be separated and processed as required.

Once you've separated the parts, tape part B and part D together. With your drill press, drill two holes through both parts using a 1" Forstner bit.

The circular cuts in part C and the switch paddle should be cut carefully, because one must rotate in the other. The better the parts fit, the less vacuum suction will be lost. Refer to the diagram for the proper shape of the switch paddle, and cut out the parts, using your scroll saw. Remember to sand a little off the face of the switch paddle

A little double-sided tape allows you to cut out parts B, C, D, E and F all together, saving you time and creating perfectly matched pieces.

Here you can see parts B, C, D, E and F after they've been cut out using the band saw.

Place all your parts in the correct order before you begin the assembly process.

to give it freedom of movement between parts B and D.

Now lay out the shape of the cutout on part E. Drill a starter hole with your drill press and then remove the waste on the inside, using a scroll saw or a jigsaw.

Now grab part F. With your drill press, drill a 1¾"-diameter hole in the location shown in the diagram.

Cut out part A, using your band saw and the diagram. Make two lead cuts from the outside profile and, still using your band saw, cut two holes sized to fit your vacuum hoses.

Finally, with either your band saw or lathe, cut or turn part G so that it will fit your particular shop vacuum's opening. Be sure to cut or sand a slight taper on part G as shown on the diagram. This taper will allow the part to fit firmly into the opening of the shop vacuum.

Here's what the unit should look like after assembly.

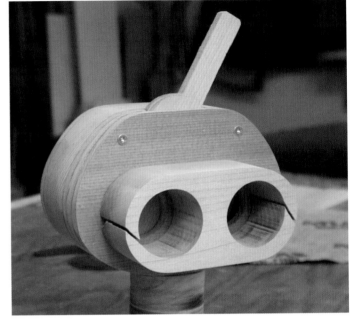

Note the "spring" saw cuts on part A. These cuts serve two purposes. First, they serve as lead cuts so the two inner holes on part A can be cut out using your band saw. Second, they provide natural spring action to allow for easy insertion of the hose ends and a tighter grip on the hose.

Here's what the unit looks like when installed on a shop vacuum.

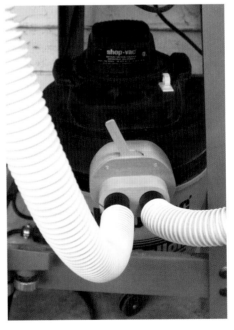

Cut out the bottoms of two 35mm film containers to connect the hose ends to the vacuum switch unit.

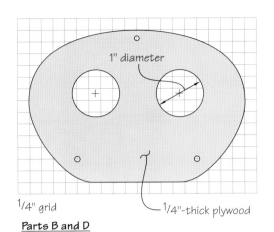

1" diameter

1/4" grid

1/4"-thick plywood

Parts B and D

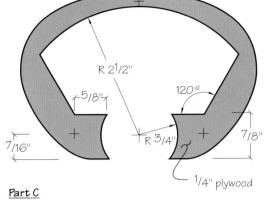

R 2¹/₂"

5/8"

120°

R ³/₄"

7/16"

7/8"

1/4" plywood

Part C

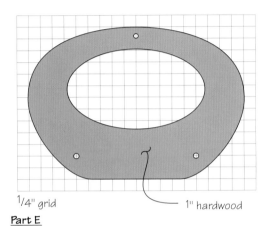

1/4" grid

1" hardwood

Part E

Part F

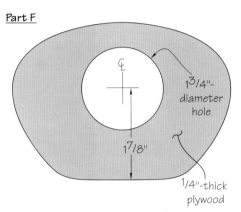

℄

1³/₄"- diameter hole

1⁷/₈"

1/4"-thick plywood

Plan View

1¹/₂"

Slight taper

Part G

1³/₄" I.D.

Approximately 2¹/₄" — make to fit your shop vacuum.

Front Elevation

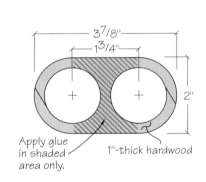

3⁷/₈"

1³/₄"

2"

Apply glue in shaded area only.

1"-thick hardwood

Part A

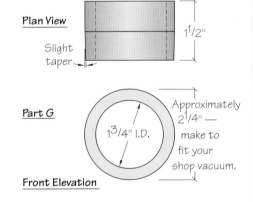

1¹/₂"

1¹/₄"

R 2⁷/₁₆"

1¹/₁₆"

R ³/₄"

This should be a snug but easily rotated fit in Part C cutout.

Make from 1/4" plywood sanded slightly thinner for easy movement when assembled.

Length to suit

1/2"

Switch Paddle

inches (millimeters)

REFERENCE	QUANTITY	PART	STOCK	THICKNESS	(mm)	WIDTH	(mm)	LENGTH	(mm)	COMMENTS
	1	part A	hardwood	1	(25)	2¹/₄	(57)	4¹/₈	(105)	
	1	part B	plywood	¹/₄	(6)	3³/₄	(95)	5¹/₄	(133)	
	1	switch paddle	plywood	¹/₄	(6)	1³/₄	(45)	6	(152)	cut to fit
	1	part C	plywood	¹/₄	(6)	3³/₄	(95)	5¹/₄	(133)	
	1	part D	plywood	¹/₄	(6)	3³/₄	(95)	5¹/₄	(133)	
	1	part E	softwood	1	(25)	3³/₄	(95)	5¹/₄	(133)	
	1	part F	plywood	¹/₄	(6)	3³/₄	(95)	5¹/₄	(133)	
	1	part G	softwood	1¹/₂	(38)	2³/₄	(70)	2³/₄	(70)	sand to fit

Note: Parts are slightly oversize to make the pattern work easier.

Final Touches

Now it's time to glue and screw the jig together. First, glue parts A and B together. Take care to apply glue on part A only as shown in the area shaded gray on the diagram. This allows for the jig's spring action.

With the switch paddle in place, screw parts B and C together. Don't use glue here in case it should ever become necessary to clear the switch paddle of debris in this area.

Now glue parts C, D, E, F and G together, making sure everything lines up properly.

When it's time to clean up the shop after a day's work, the unit can be easily popped out of the shop vacuum and the regular hose inserted. Now you can add permanent dust collection to your two favorite machines without the expense of an extensive piping and exhaust system.

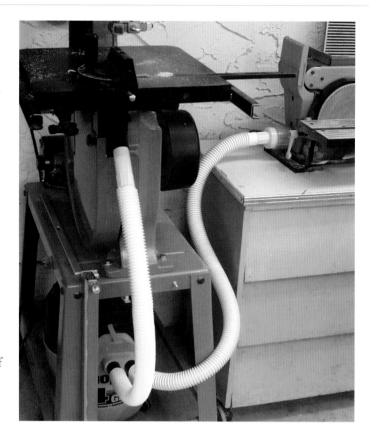

I've placed my shop vacuum under my band saw and next to my sander. A flip of the switch paddle and my dust is under control, no matter which machine I use.

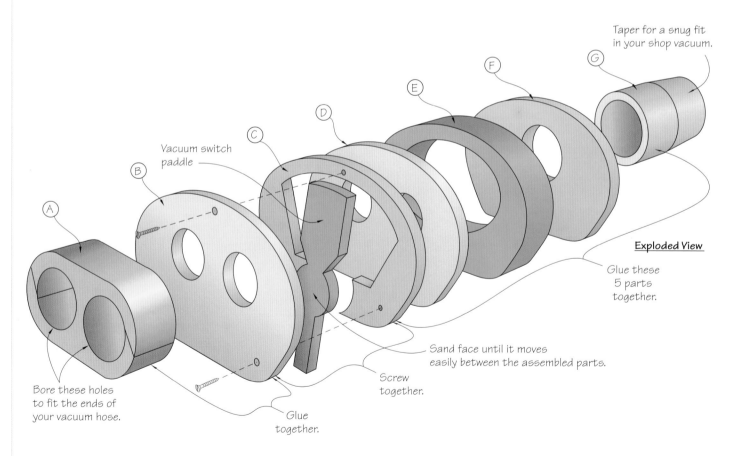

Taper for a snug fit in your shop vacuum.

Vacuum switch paddle

Exploded View

Glue these 5 parts together.

Sand face until it moves easily between the assembled parts.

Screw together.

Glue together.

Bore these holes to fit the ends of your vacuum hose.

Clamp Assist

Simple solutions to three perplexing assembly problems.

BY NICK ENGLER

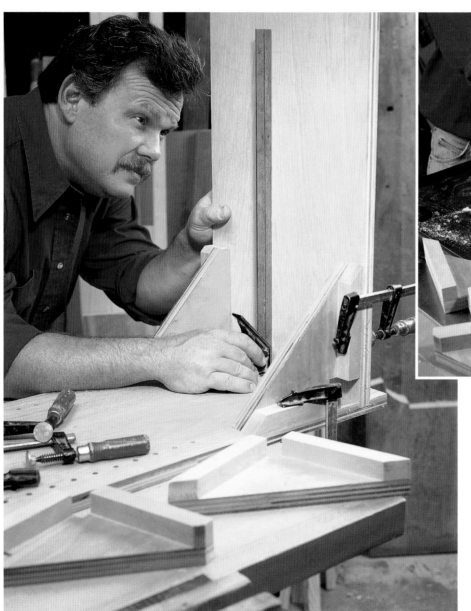

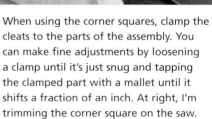

When using the corner squares, clamp the cleats to the parts of the assembly. You can make fine adjustments by loosening a clamp until it's just snug and tapping the clamped part with a mallet until it shifts a fraction of an inch. At right, I'm trimming the corner square on the saw.

Most woodworkers operate under the theory that you can't have too many clamps, and stock them by the dozens, even the hundreds. I'm one of those, I admit. My clamp inventory takes up a whole corner of my shop — when my shop is straightened up, that is. On most days, my clamp collection is spread out over the entire shop so I can enjoy it properly.

For all my clamps, however, I frequently run across assembly tasks that I can't do properly with store-bought clamping equipment alone. For these tasks, I've developed several simple "clamp assists" that extend the capabilities of ordinary clamps to help accomplish extraordinary clamping jobs.

Holding Assembled Parts Square

When assembling projects, you frequently need to hold the parts square to one another. Miter clamps have their place, but they aren't as versatile or as easy to use as corner squares. These simple jigs are triangular pieces of plywood with cleats along the edges at right angles to one another. You clamp the cleats to the parts you are assembling, and the corner squares hold them at 90°.

To make the corner squares, first cut right triangles from ³/₄" plywood. Note that I put a little notch in the right-angle corner. When you glue the parts together, sometimes a little glue squeezes out of the joint. The notch prevents the glue from sticking the jig to the assembly. Attach cleats to the right-angle sides, then trim the cleats on a table saw to make sure the outside edges are precisely 90° from one another.

These jigs are useful for dozens of shop chores. They also will hold temporary assemblies together while you test the fit of the parts. They hold boards together while you drill holes for fasteners, or hold the parts of a frame or a box square to one another while the glue dries. I have even used them to hold large boards — too large to fit in a vise — while I worked the ends or edges.

Here I'm setting up to clamp two boards face to face.

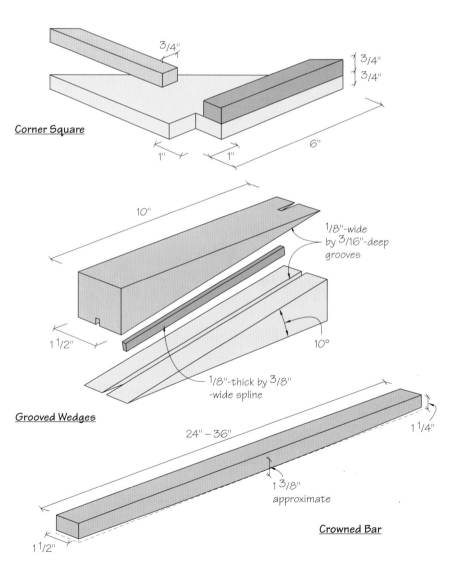

Corner Square

3/4"

3/4"
3/4"

1"   1"

6"

Grooved Wedges

10"

1 1/2"

1/8"-wide by 3/16"-deep grooves

10°

1/8"-thick by 3/8"-wide spline

Crowned Bar

24" – 36"

1 1/4"

1 3/8" approximate

1 1/2"

Clamping Face-to-Face

Occasionally, I need to clamp two boards face-to-face. This is a simple chore when the boards are narrow, but it becomes more difficult as the boards grow wider. Even deep-throated clamps have a limited capacity that may not reach to the center of wide boards. Consequently, you won't get an even clamping pressure all across the width, and the assembly will be weak in the center. You run into a similar problem when trying to attach veneer or marquetry to a wide panel. How do you clamp the center area?

For years, I solved the problem by keeping a stack of concrete blocks outside the shop. When I needed pressure in the center of a wide assembly, I stacked blocks on it. It works, but it's inconvenient and somewhat limited.

A better solution is to make a set of crowned bars. These are hardwood bars, 24" to 36" long, with one convex edge. This edge is crowned only slightly, about $1/16$" to $1/8$" wider in the center than it is at the ends. I cut a crown by raising the outfeed table of my jointer a few thousandths of an inch above the knives and jointing the edge. You can also create a crown with a band saw, a hand plane or a disc sander.

To use the crowned bars, lay the assembly on a flat workbench and lay the bars across the assembly with the crowned edge down. (I label the opposite edge with the word *up* to help me orient the bars properly.) Then clamp the ends of the bars to the workbench. The bars will flex slightly, evenly distributing the pressure from the middle out to the edges of the assembly.

Applying Tension

Clamps are designed, by and large, to generate compression to squeeze two boards together. But every now and then, you need some tension either to pull an assembled joint apart or to clamp a part inside a larger assembly. When I need a little tension, I rely on a set of grooved wedges.

I cut the wedges from a hardwood with a slope of about 10°. If the slope is any steeper than that, you run the risk of the wedges slipping when you use

I'm trimming the corner square on the saw. Lay the crowned bars across the assembly with the crowned edges down. Then, clamp the ends of the bars to the workbench.

Grooved wedges are useful not only for putting projects together but also for taking them apart. Here I'm using the wedges to pop the joints of a wobbly chair as I prepare to restore it.

them. Make a groove in each sloping edge by cutting a shallow saw kerf down the center. Finally, make a spline to fit the kerfs. The spline should be as thick as the kerf is wide and twice as wide as the kerf is deep.

To use the wedges, position them slope-to-slope with the spline in the grooves. Use a bar clamp to slide the wedges together so each wedge climbs the other's slope. As this happens, the outside edges of the wedges will push against the parts of the assembly, applying tension.

Cold Bending the Wright Way

Cold bending is a whole lot easier with this flexible clamping fixture.

BY NICK ENGLER

In my mind, there are three classifications of woodworking techniques: Many that I classify as "useful," a smaller number that I think of as "indispensable," and then a very few that represent a true breakthrough in woodworking technology. Bending wood is one of the latter.

The ability to alter the grain direction as our imagination dictates while preserving the strength inherent in a straight piece of wood allows us to create the elegant beauty of a continuous-arm Windsor chair and the inspiring sweep of a vaulted ceiling. We first explored our world in sailing ships with bentwood hulls, then left it in airplanes with bentwood wings. Our world would be much less beautiful and much less exciting without this simple woodworking technique.

I'm currently engaged in a woodworking project designed to create a little excitement, and bending wood is at the very heart of it. I'm part of a group of historians and aviators who are recreating the six experimental airplanes of the Wright brothers, beginning with their model glider of 1899 and ending with the 1905 Wright Flyer 3, the first practical airplane. The frames of these primitive aircraft are a collection of bentwood parts — ribs, wing ends, braces and skids — ingeniously arranged to catch the wind and lift a man into the air.

True Geniuses Prefer Cold Bending

When most of us hear the words *bending wood*, we think of steam bending. The wood is heated briefly in low-pressure steam to soften the lignin (a gluelike protein that holds the cellulose fibers together). While the wood is still hot, it's clamped into a bending form. The cellulose fibers telescope to conform to the curve, and the lignin cools to hold them in place. Or almost. In actual practice, the fibers never quite conform, and when you remove the wood from the bending form, there is a great deal of springback; the wood loses some of its curve. If the wood is not attached to the other parts in the project so as to hold the curve, it may continue to relax and it will spring back even more. This problem plagued the Wright brothers while they were doing their glider experiments: They calculated precise curves for the ribs to fly as efficiently as possible, only to have the ribs relax and lose a good deal of curvature before they could get their gliders in the air.

To solve this problem, they eventually abandoned steam bending for an early form of cold bending. They arranged the parts of the ribs for their Flyers in a bending form, then nailed them together with brads. They could not use glue; the adhesives 100 years ago were not weatherproof. A good rain and the wings would have come apart.

Fortunately, we have a much larger and more reliable selection of adhesives to choose from than the Wrights did. We decided to make the bentwood ribs of our replica Wright gliders by laminating the parts with a water-resistant aliphatic resin (yellow) glue. You could also use resorcinol, epoxy or polyurethane glue for an application like ours. If your project won't be exposed to the weather, you can use almost any good wood glue.

To cold-bend wood, first resaw your stock into thin strips and plane it so the thickness is even. The thickness of the strips depends to a large extent on the radius of the curve. The tighter the radius, the thinner the strips. I use this chart as a jumping-off point:

- 2" to 4" radius — $3/32$" thick
- 4" to 8" radius — $1/8$" thick
- 8" to 12" radius — $3/16$" thick
- 12" radius or larger — $1/4$" thick

There are other factors to consider: the species of wood, the slope of the grain (as it runs between the faces of the strips), the strength you want and the amount of springback you can tolerate. For maximum strength and minimum springback, we decided to glue up the ribs from $1/8$"-thick strips, although the radius of the curve was nowhere near 8".

Stack the strips as you will glue them together. If you use strips that were all resawn from the same board, flip every other strip end for end to reverse the grain slope. Spread a thin layer of glue on the face of one strip, lay the next strip on top of it, spread more glue and repeat. If you're laminating a large number of strips, you may want to choose an adhesive with an extended working time.

Before the glue sets, clamp the laminated strip in the bending form. Let the glue set up for its full clamp time. If you're not sure of the clamp time, wait a full day before you remove the assembly from the bending form. As you release the clamps, there will be a small amount of springback. If the curve is critical (as it was for our glider ribs), make the curves in the bending form slightly tighter to compensate.

Making a Cold-Bending Form

Pretty simple, huh? The only real trick to cold bending is in making a form that will apply an even clamping pressure all along the laminated assembly. Traditional bending forms consist of two parts; the form (the positive shape) and the press (the negative shape). Both of these parts are normally cut from the same stock. Begin by drawing the curve you want on the face of the stock. Cut the curve with a band saw, separating the stock into two parts. On the negative part, mark the thickness of the bentwood part. Tip: Use a compass like calipers and set it to the desired thickness and follow the curve with

Spread the glue on the surface of each strip with a $3/8$"–32 threaded rod to draw the adhesive out as evenly as possible. Note that I've placed the strip on a long scrap to elevate it above the bench. This allows the extra glue to drip over the edge.

Clamp the laminated strips in the bending form, spacing the clamps every 3" — dead center of each segment of the press. I drilled $1\frac{1}{4}$"-diameter holes in the form to hold the top face of the clamps and automatically space them.

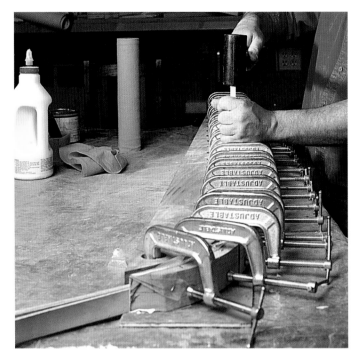

Before you tighten the clamps, just snug them up to hold the stock against the form. With a scrap of wood and a hammer, tap the top edges of the strips to even them up. Then tighten the clamps until the gaps disappear between the laminations.

the point of the compass, marking the thickness with the scribe. Cut away the thickness on the band saw; this will create the press.

The trouble with this traditional bending form is that the press doesn't compensate for small variations in the thickness of the laminated stock or a band saw blade that wanders a hair off the line. Consequently, when you apply the clamps, the clamping pressure may not be completely even all along the form. This may result in weak laminations or even in gaps between the laminations when the glue dries.

To ensure that this didn't happen to our glider ribs, I designed a compensat-ing press. After cutting away the thickness of the bentwood part, use the compass to mark yet another curve on the negative part, this one 1" larger in radius than the curve you just cut. Saw this curve, then cut the 1"-thick piece into 3"-long segments. Adhere the segments back to the negative part temporarily with double-faced carpet tape. Glue a strip of canvas to the inside curve of the segments and cover the canvas with 6-mil plastic.

When you separate the segments from the negative part and discard the tape, they should be held together by the canvas like the tambours of a rolltop desk. This is your press. When you squeeze the laminated stock to the form, arrange the clamps in the middle of each segment; this will compensate for any variation in stock thickness or inaccuracies in the bending form and keep the clamping pressure relatively even.

Note: The plastic on the press will keep any glue that squeezes out between the laminations from sticking to the canvas. To prevent the squeeze-out from sticking to the form, apply paste wax to the form before each glue-up.

Spreading the Glue

Just as uneven clamping pressure will reduce the strength of the lamination, so will an uneven application of glue. You must spread it as evenly as possible, and I've got just the ticket. This little trick was shown to me by the good folks at Franklin International (makers of Titebond glue). Get rid of your glue brushes and spread the glue with the teeth of a $3/8$"–32 threaded rod. The threads spread the glue to just the right thickness (about 0.005") for a strong joint with a minimum of squeeze-out. For this particular project, I mounted a short length of threaded rod in a wooden handle. Between glue-ups, I keep the rod submersed in water to prevent the glue from drying on the threads.

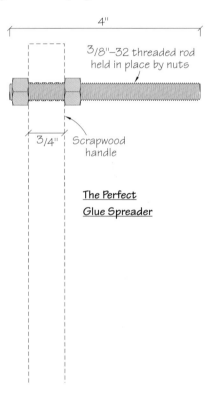

4"

$3/8$"–32 threaded rod held in place by nuts

$3/4$" Scrapwood handle

The Perfect
Glue Spreader

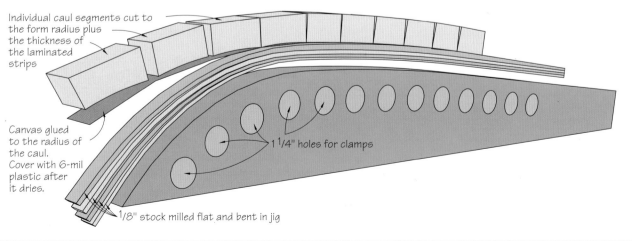

Individual caul segments cut to the form radius plus the thickness of the laminated strips

Canvas glued to the radius of the caul. Cover with 6-mil plastic after it dries.

1 1/4" holes for clamps

1/8" stock milled flat and bent in jig

PROJECT

34

Microadjustable Support Stand

The extra hand you need — and one more.

BY NICK ENGLER

My grandfather used to call them "dead men" — T-shaped stands that he placed outboard of a tool or a workbench for additional support. They were the extra hands he needed to manage large workpieces — when I wasn't around, that is. After I was old enough to have my own shop, I built dead men topped with rollers to help support the work. These roller stands are very useful — indispensable, really, unless you have a permanent grandchild installed in your shop.

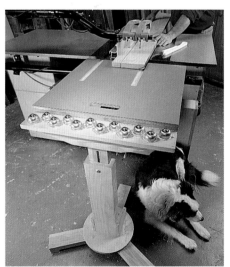

To adjust the extension table level with the tool, lay a straightedge across them. Loosen the locking knob and raise the roller head. It's so easy, you're guaranteed not to curse and wake Fluffy.

115

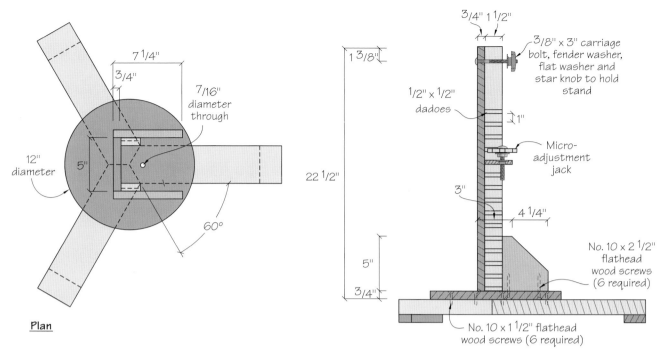

Plan

3/4" 1 1/2"

1 3/8"

3/8" x 3" carriage
bolt, fender washer,
flat washer and
star knob to hold
stand

1/2" x 1/2"
dadoes

1"

Micro-
adjustment
jack

22 1/2"

3"

4 1/4"

No. 10 x 2 1/2"
flathead
wood screws
(6 required)

5"

3/4"

No. 10 x 1 1/2" flathead
wood screws (6 required)

Profile

The trouble is, sometimes a board droops as it leaves the worktable. By the time it reaches the stand, it may have dropped below the roller. You need a grandchild to guide the workpiece onto the stand, which, of course, puts you right back to square one.

Because my own grandchildren are not all that useful yet (they still tend to drool on the tools), I decided to improve my roller stand by adding an extension table. This table fills the gap between the stand and the worktable, supporting the workpiece and guiding it onto the rollers. It's an extra hand for my extra hand, if you will. When I don't need the table, it swings down out of the way, and I can use the roller stand alone.

I made one more improvement. When using a support stand or an extension table, it's difficult to adjust it level with the power tool. So I made this stand microadjustable. A small screw jack makes it possible to dial in the position of the stand and the table in $\frac{1}{64}$" increments. Pretty neat, huh? You can't get this option elsewhere, even on the better grade of grandkids.

Building the Support Stand

The support stand is made up of four assemblies: the base, the roller head, the extension table and the microadjustment jack.

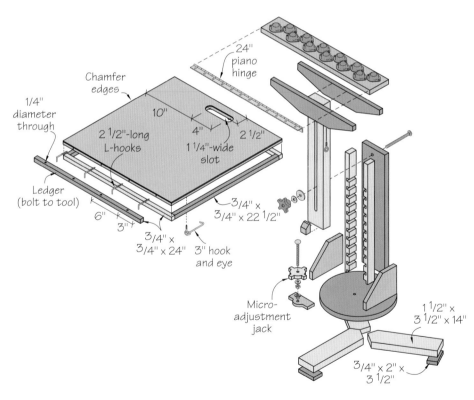

Chamfer
edges

24"
piano
hinge

1/4"
diameter
through

10"

4"

2 1/2"

2 1/2"-long
L-hooks

1 1/4"-wide
slot

Ledger
(bolt to tool)

3/4" x
3/4" x 22 1/2"

6"

3"

3/4" x
3/4" x 24"

3" hook
and eye

Micro-
adjustment
jack

1 1/2" x
3 1/2" x 14"

3/4" x 2" x
3 1/2"

HARDWARE

1" (25mm)   ball bearing work rollers   item #07B08   Woodcraft

116

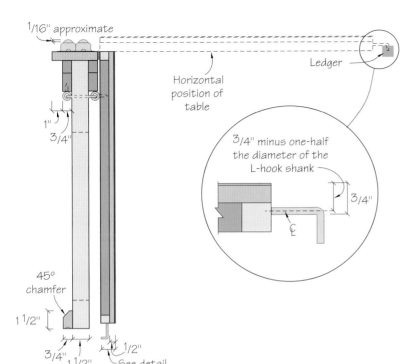

To use the roller stand alone, simply swing the extension table down out of the way.

Elevation

Base. The base rests on three feet so it will be stable, even on an uneven floor. The feet support a U-shaped channel that holds the roller head and guides it up and down. The sides of this channel are dadoed to hold the microadjustment jack.

To make the base, double-miter the adjoining ends of the legs and attach them to the underside of a round plywood plate with screws and glue. Cut dadoes in a board spaced every 1", then rip the board into two strips. Use these strips for the sides of the U-shaped guide. Assemble the guide and attach it to the top of the round plate.

Roller Head. To help feed the work across the stand, I used 1" ball bearing work rollers (sometimes called roller bearings or transfer balls). I like these doodads because they will roll in any direction. You can use them to rip, crosscut or cut circles without having to worry about the roller pulling the work to one side if it isn't perfectly aligned with the direction of feed.

I arranged the rollers in two staggered rows on the top of a T-shaped mount. This arrangement packs the balls closer together and gives you

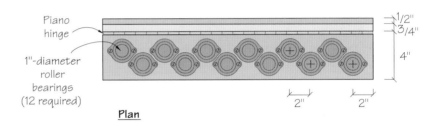

Plan

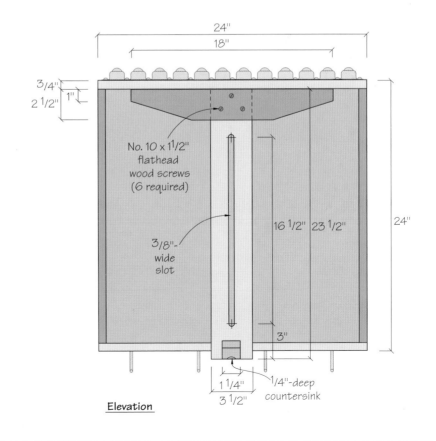

Elevation

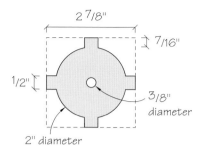

2 7/8"

7/16"

1/2"

3/8" diameter

2" diameter

Jack Top Layout

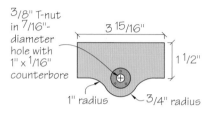

3/8" T-nut in 7/16"-diameter hole with 1" x 1/16" counterbore

3 15/16"

1 1/2"

1" radius   3/4" radius

Jack Base Layout

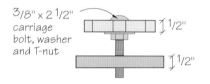

3/8" x 2 1/2" carriage bolt, washer and T-nut

1/2"

1/2"

Jack Side View

Insert the microadjustment jack into the dado slots just below the post. Let the post drop down onto the jack, then turn the knob until you can't see any daylight between the table and the straightedge.

more support when feeding narrow workpieces.

Rout a long slot down the center of the post that supports the roller head. When the post is mounted in the base, a carriage bolt extends through the post slot and the back of the guide. A star knob and a fender washer secure the post in the guide. To adjust the height of the stand, loosen the knob.

As drawn, the support stand adjusts from 30" to 46 1/2" high — just a little lower and a little higher than the tools in my shop. If it doesn't work for your shop, you can change the height range by varying the length of the guide, post and slot.

Extension Table. The table is just a 1/2"-thick piece of plywood. I mounted the plywood to 3/4" frame members to stiffen it and covered the top with plastic laminate to prevent the surface from wearing.

One end of the extension table is attached to the roller head with a piano hinge. Screw the hinge to the table first, then position it on the roller head. Have a grandkid hold the table out horizontal

while you move the hinge until the tops of the roller bearings are 1/16" above the top of the table. Clamp the hinge to the roller head and secure it with screws.

The other end of the table hooks to a ledger. This is a one-by with a few holes in it. Bolt the ledger to the side of the machine or bench where you want to attach the support stand. The top face of the ledger should be precisely 3/4" below the work surface. Install L-hooks in the end of the table, spaced the same as the holes in the ledger. The hooks fit in the ledger, securing the table. You can fine-tune the height of the table by bending the hooks.

I've made several ledgers and attached them to the tools where I use the support stand. I've attached two ledgers to my table saw — one for ripping and one for crosscutting. This lets me move the stand wherever it's needed.

Cut a slot in the table to serve as a handhold to carry the stand around the shop. To keep the table from flipping up when you do this, install a hook and eye in the underside of the roller head and the extension table.

Microadjustment Jack. The jack is just a carriage bolt that turns in a T-nut. The T-nut rests in a small base that's slightly wider than the post and thinner than the dadoes in the guide. This lets you slide it in and out of the dadoes whenever you must readjust the height of the stand. The head of the carriage bolt is embedded in a wooden knob with several tabs around the circumference. These tabs not only help you turn the knob, they allow you to calculate precisely how much you're raising or lowering the roller head and extension table.

The carriage bolt is 3/8"–16 — which is 16 threads per inch. Turn it just one revolution and you raise or lower the stand 1/16". One-quarter turn (one tab) moves the stand 1/64".

The top of the carriage bolt butts against a small wooden "finger" that is glued to face of the post, flush with the bottom. I drilled a shallow countersink in the bottom of this finger. The domed head of the carriage bolt rests in this countersink. This, in turn, keeps the bolt from wandering or wobbling as you turn the knob.

Sandpaper-Cutting Jig

Tear into your sanding with this jig.

BY JIM STACK

This is a simple jig for cutting 9" × 11" sheets of sandpaper into four $4\frac{1}{2}$" × $5\frac{1}{2}$" sheets. This size is perfect for folding in half and using for hand sanding or wrapping around a $\frac{3}{4}$" × $2\frac{3}{4}$" × $5\frac{1}{2}$" sanding block.

To use, insert the full sheet of sandpaper in the $5\frac{1}{2}$" side of the jig and tear the sheet in half. Insert one of these halves in the $4\frac{1}{2}$" side and tear that half in half.

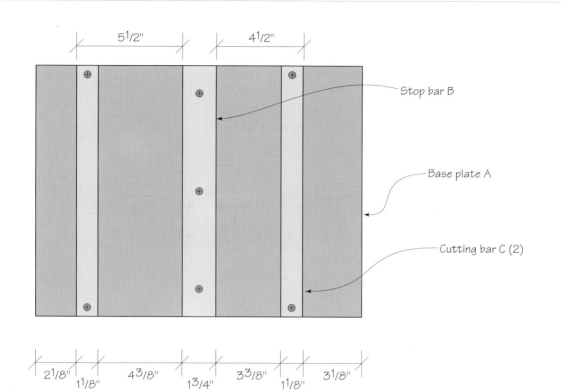

5¹/₂"   4¹/₂"

Stop bar B

Base plate A

Cutting bar C (2)

2¹/₈"   1¹/₈"   4³/₈"   1³/₄"   3³/₈"   1¹/₈"   3¹/₈"

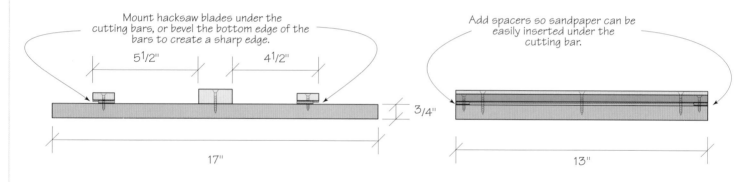

Mount hacksaw blades under the cutting bars, or bevel the bottom edge of the bars to create a sharp edge.

Add spacers so sandpaper can be easily inserted under the cutting bar.

5¹/₂"   4¹/₂"

3/4"

17"

13"

REFERENCE	QUANTITY	PART	STOCK	THICKNESS	(mm)	WIDTH	(mm)	LENGTH	(mm)
A	1	base plate	plywood	3/4	(19)	13	(330)	17	(432)
B	1	stop bar	hardwood	3/4	(19)	1³/₄	(45)	13	(330)
C	2	cutting bars	hardwood	3/8	(10)	1¹/₈	(29)	13	(330)

HARDWARE

3   No. 8 × 1¹/₄" (No. 8 × 32mm) flathead wood screws

4   No. 6 × 1" (No. 6 × 25mm) flathead wood screws

2   hacksaw blades

4   thin cardboard shims for spacing the cutter bars

PROJECT

36

Shim-Making Fixture

Make great wedges in 3 minutes.

BY JIM STACK

I've discovered that shims (or wedges) are a great tool to have around the shop. From leveling power tools to a quick pad for a clamp, shims can come in handy.

This fixture is easy to make and safe to use. Cut the shim shape in the bottom using a band saw, jigsaw or hand saw. (See the illustration for details.) If you want a longer shim with a shallower rise, adjust the shim-shape cut in the bottom.

When using the shim maker, raise the table saw blade until it is about $1/16$" higher than the bottom of the shim maker.

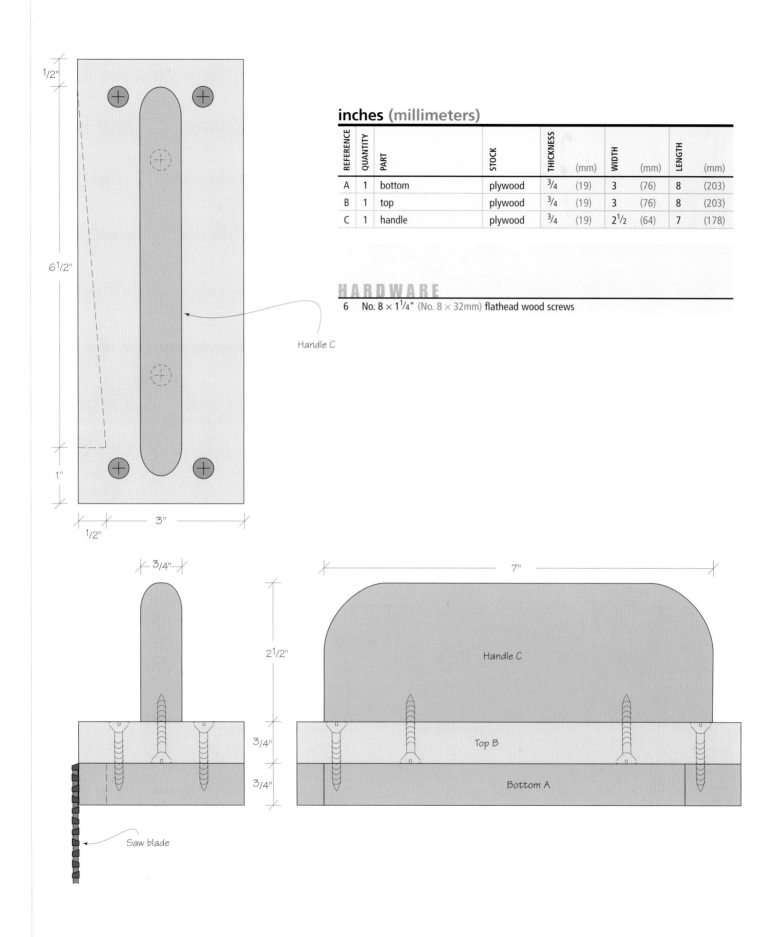

Handle C

inches (millimeters)

REFERENCE	QUANTITY	PART	STOCK	THICKNESS	(mm)	WIDTH	(mm)	LENGTH	(mm)
A	1	bottom	plywood	3/4	(19)	3	(76)	8	(203)
B	1	top	plywood	3/4	(19)	3	(76)	8	(203)
C	1	handle	plywood	3/4	(19)	2½	(64)	7	(178)

HARDWARE

6 No. 8 × 1¼" (No. 8 × 32mm) flathead wood screws

Top B

Bottom A

Saw blade

Two Versions of a Beam Compass

Draw circles and arcs with a single stroke.

BY JIM STACK

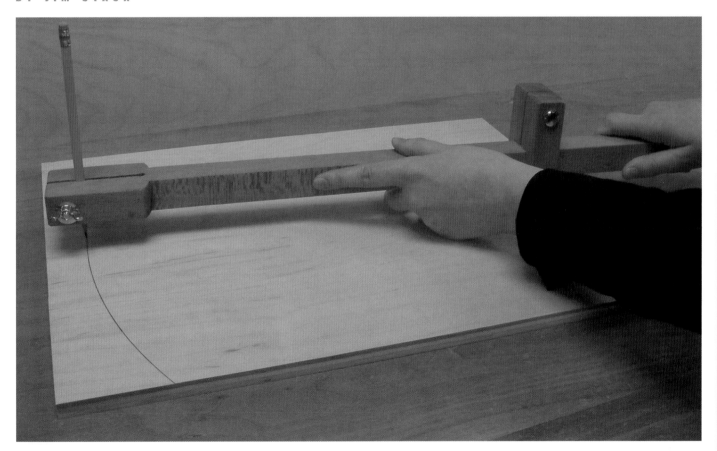

This beam compass is not a new idea or design, but it's a good one. A set of trammel points can cost as much as a set of chisels, so by building this beam compass you can get a set of chisels for free — well, sort of.

To make version No. 1, cut out all the parts as shown in the materials list. Then, cut a ⅛"-wide slot in one end of the beam. Shape two of the wings to whatever shape you desire, then glue them to the slotted end of the beam. Put a spacer or wedge in the slot to keep it from compressing when you clamp the wings.

Using the beam as a spacer, glue the pivot assembly together. When the glue has dried, shape the assembly to your desired shape. Then cut the slot in the longer filler, using the same method as you cut the slot in the beam.

Use a drill press to bore a hole at the termination of the slot in the beam. This will prevent the beam from splitting. Then bore the hole for the pencil. Finally, bore both holes for the carriage bolts.

Sand and finish with wax. Then start drawing circles.

Set the fence on your band saw so it cuts just off center of the beam. Make a cut, then flip the beam over and make another cut the same length as the first cut. Move the fence a little and enlarge the groove to 1/8" wide. Use this same technique to cut the groove in the adjustable center assembly on compass version No. 1.

This is the end of the beam and the adjustable center on compass version No. 1. Note the 1/8"-thick stiffener strip at the bottom of the square cutout on the center assembly. This will keep the assembly from splitting.

The easiest way to create the groove in this compass is to glue a spacer at each end of the beams. After the glue dries, cut the ends smooth, cut the slot in the end, drill the two holes, install the center pin assembly and you're good to go.

Version No. 2 is made using the same techniques as used to make version No. 1. Drill the knob for a T-nut. Cut the head off of the second carriage bolt and use the threaded rod to make the center guide for the compass. Grind one end of the rod to a point, then thread two nuts onto the rod and turn them against each other to lock them in place. Install the T-nut in the knob and thread the knob onto the rod/nut assembly.

This is what compass version No. 2 looks like. It is easier to make than version No. 1. Either version will work well when drawing circles.

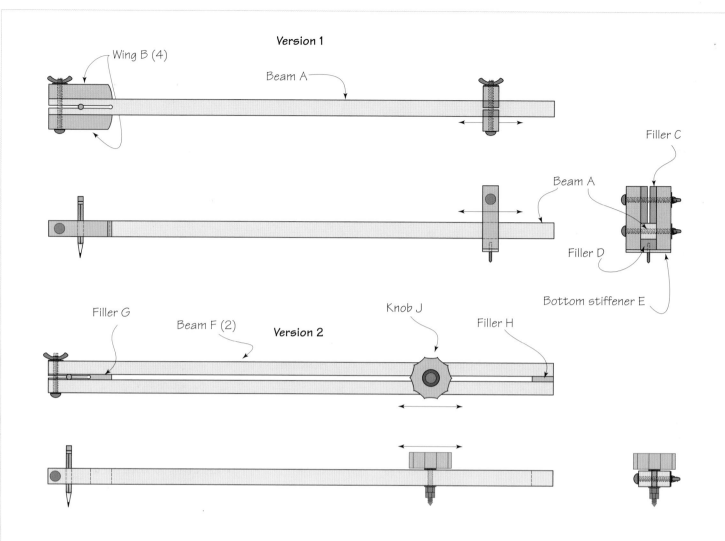

Version 1

Wing B (4)

Beam A

Beam A

Filler C

Filler D

Bottom stiffener E

Filler G

Beam F (2)

Version 2

Knob J

Filler H

Beam Compass No. 1 — inches (millimeters)

REFERENCE	QUANTITY	PART	STOCK	THICKNESS	(mm)	WIDTH	(mm)	LENGTH	(mm)
A	1	beam	hardwood	1	(25)	1	(25)	24	(610)
B	4	wings	hardwood	3/4	(19)	3/4	(19)	3	(76)
C	1	filler	hardwood	1	(25)	1	(25)	1 3/4	(45)
D	1	filler	hardwood	1	(25)	1	(25)	1/2	(13)
E	1	bottom stiffener	hardwood	1/8	(3)	1	(25)	2 1/8	(54)

HARDWARE

2 2 1/2" × 1/4"–20 (64mm × 6mm–20) carriage bolts
2 1/4" (6mm) flat washers
2 1/4" (6mm) wing nuts
1 6d finishing nail (cut to length)

Beam Compass No. 2 — inches (millimeters)

REFERENCE	QUANTITY	PART	STOCK	THICKNESS	(mm)	WIDTH	(mm)	LENGTH	(mm)
F	2	beams	hardwood	5/8	(16)	1	(25)	24	(610)
G	1	filler	hardwood	1/4	(6)	1	(25)	3	(76)
H	1	filler	hardwood	1/4	(6)	1	(25)	1	(25)
J	1	knob	plywood	3/4	(19)	2 dia	(51)		

HARDWARE

2 2 1/2" × 1/4"–20 (64mm × 6mm–20) carriage bolts
3 1/4" (6mm) flat washers
1 1/4" (6mm) wing nut
1 1/4"–20 (6mm–20) T-nut

SUPPLIERS

ADAMS & KENNEDY — THE WOODSOURCE
6178 Mitch Owen Road
P.O. Box 700
Manotick, Ontario, Canada K4M 1A6
613-822-6800
www.wood-source.com
Wood supply

B&Q
B&Q Head Office
Portswood House
1 Hampshire Corporate Park
Chandlers Ford
Eastleigh
Hampshire
SO53 3YX
023 8025 6256
www.diy.com
Tools, paint, wood, electrical, garden

CRAFTSMAN
Sears
800-549-4504
www.craftsman.com
Craftsman tools

FREUD TOOLS
218 Feld Avenue
High Point, North Carolina 27263
800-334-4107
www.freudtools.com
Carbide-tipped saw blades, dado sets, tooling

GARRETT WADE
161 Avenue of the Americas
New York, New York 10013
800-221-2942
www.garrettwade.com
General hand tools and supplies, power tools

THE HOME DEPOT
Attention: Customer Care
2455 Paces Ferry Road
Atlanta, Georgia 30339
800-553-3199 (U.S.)
800-668-2266 (Canada)
www.homedepot.com
Tools, paint, wood, electrical, garden

HOUSE OF TOOLS LTD.
100 Mayfield Common Northwest
Edmonton, Alberta, Canada T5P 4B3
800-661-3987
www.houseoftools.com
Woodworking tools and hardware

LEE VALLEY TOOLS LTD.
U.S.:
P.O. Box 1780
Ogdensburg, New York 13669-6780
800-267-8735
Canada:
P.O. Box 6295, Station J
Ottawa, Ontario, Canada K2A 1T4
800-267-8761
www.leevalley.com
Woodworking tools and hardware

LOWE'S HOME IMPROVEMENT WAREHOUSE
P.O. Box 1111
North Wilkesboro, North Carolina 28656
800-445-6937
www.lowes.com
Tools, paint, wood, electrical, garden

MICRO-SURFACE FINISHING PRODUCTS, INC.
1217 West Third Street
Wilton, Iowa 52778
800-225-3006
www.micro-surface.com
Abrasives and finishing products

PAXTON WOODCRAFTERS' STORE
4837 Jackson Street
Denver, Colorado 80216
800-332-1331
www.paxton-woodsource.com
*Domestic and foreign hardwoods; veneers;
books and woodworking tools*

PORTER-CABLE
4825 Highway 45 North
P.O. Box 2468
Jackson, Tennessee 38302-2468
800-487-8665
www.porter-cable.com
Woodworking tools

REID TOOL SUPPLY COMPANY
2265 Black Creek Road
Muskegon, Michigan 49441
800-253-0421
www.reidtool.com
Woodworking hardware and accessories

RICHELIEU HARDWARE
7900, West Henri-Bourassa
Ville St-Laurent, Quebec, Canada
H4S 1V4
800-619-5446 (U.S.)
800-361-6000 (Canada)
www.richelieu.com
Hardware supplies

ROCKLER WOODWORKING AND HARDWARE
4365 Willow Drive
Medina, Minnesota 55340
800-279-4441
www.rockler.com
Woodworking tools and hardware

WOLFCRAFT NORTH AMERICA
1222 West Ardmore Avenue
P.O. Box 687
Itasca, Illinois 60143
630-773-4777
www.wolfcraft.com
Woodworking hardware and accessories

WOODCRAFT
P.O. Box 1686
Parkersburg, West Virginia 26102-1686
800-225-1153
www.woodcraft.com
Woodworking hardware and accessories

WOODWORKER'S SUPPLY, INC.
Attention: Order Dept.
1108 North Glenn Road
Casper, Wyoming 82601
800-645-9292
www.woodworker.com
Woodworking tools and supplies

INDEX